~TE DUE

Renner Learning Resource Center
Elgin Community College
Elgin, IL 60123

VGM Opportunities Series

OPPORTUNITIES IN **MEDICAL SALES CAREERS**

Chad Ellis

.Foreword by
Kevin Whelan
Marketing Manager
Hill-Rom Long Term Care

 **VGM Career Horizons**
a division of *NTC Publishing Group*
Lincolnwood, Illinois USA

RENNER LEARNING RESOURCE CENTER
ELGIN COMMUNITY COLLEGE
ELGIN, ILLINOIS 60123

Cover Photo Credits

All photos courtesy of Bristol-Myers Squibb Company, Princeton, New Jersey.

Library of Congress Cataloging-in-Publication Date

Ellis, Chad Wayne.
 Opportunities in medical sales careers / Chad Wayne Ellis.
  p. cm. — (VGM opportunities series)
 Includes index.
 ISBN 0-8442-4560-7 (alk. paper). — ISBN 0-8442-4561-5 (pbk. :
alk. paper)
 1. Medical instruments and apparatus industry—Vocational
guidance—United States. 2. Pharmaceutical industry—Vocational
guidance—United States. 3. Medical supplies industry—Vocational
guidance—United States. 4. Selling—Vocational guidance—United
States. I. Title. II. Series.
HD9994.U52E45 1997
681'.761'0688—dc21   96-45333
                                                              CIP

Published by VGM Career Horizons, a division of NTC Publishing Group
4255 West Touhy Avenue
Lincolnwood (Chicago), Illinois 60646-1975, U.S.A.
© 1997 by NTC Publishing Group. All rights reserved.
No part of this book may be reproduced, stored in a retrieval
system, or transmitted in any form or by any means,
electronic, mechanical, photocopying, recording or otherwise,
without the prior permission of NTC Publishing Group.
Manufactured in the United States of America.

7 8 9 0 VP 9 8 7 6 5 4 3 2 1

CONTENTS

ABOUT THE AUTHOR

Chad Ellis began his career in medical sales in 1982 when he accepted a sales position with the Procter & Gamble company in their surgical products division. After four years with that company, he joined the Professional Health Care division of Kimberly-Clark. During his tenure with both companies, Mr. Ellis has worked as a sales representative, sales trainer, corporate recruiter, and sales manager. In his eleven years with Kimberly-Clark, he has held four sales positions and currently holds the position of Account Executive.

In his duties at Kimberly-Clark, Mr. Ellis has trained seventy-five medical representatives in six countries while maintaining direct account responsibility for seventy-five health care accounts. He currently gives more than 100 educational in-services annually in Kimberly-Clark's Excellence in Sterile Processing series, has been the number one sales representative in the company, serves on the sales advisory board, and is a member of the Value Task Team, which is dedicated to educating and training hospital staff members on new methods of cost reduction.

Mr. Ellis earned his bachelor of arts degree in communications and math from Western Kentucky University in 1981 and has also completed the necessary course work toward a master's degree in organizational communication.

ACKNOWLEDGMENTS

This book was written as a result of my lifelong experiences in medical sales, but each experience has always been shaped by the influence of others. In the fifteen years since I first started, I have been fortunate to meet hundreds of sales representatives and managers who have shaped my vision of this career field. I have also been privileged to work with caring customers who have made the job both challenging and rewarding.

First, I am grateful to my very first sales trainer, David Hoke, who demonstrated by example what it means to be professional. His thorough approach to product knowledge and customer follow up set the stage for my personal sales development and gave me a love for the job that has never diminished.

Next, I greatly appreciate the contributions made over the years by my friend and business associate, Jim Destino. His ability to assess people and business situations accurately has always been a talent that I have wished for and would love to borrow. Jim's sales and management philosophies and entrepreneurial spirit encouraged me to write this book.

I also want to express my thanks to some of my sales peers who have inspired me through the years. Mark Kellerman, Cindy Mette, and Betty Roberts are all consummate professionals whose judgment I have always trusted and whose sales performance I have always respected.

Finally, I want to thank my wife, Joyce, for her encouragement to write the book and for her constant search to do everything just a little better than it has been done before. Also, great thanks to my wonderful children, Emily and Olivia, who are the reason I get up and go out the door every day. Thank you all!

FOREWORD

Learning the job of a medical sales professional is a tough task. For me, it was made tougher by having no basic information while I tried to learn. Consequently, my learning was characterized by one misunderstanding after another.

I knew nothing about medical sales when I went to interview for a logistics position with the old American Hospital Supply Company. The interviewer horrified me by suggesting that my personality might best be suited for sales. Up to that point, my only exposure to sales had been the "snake oil" salespeople portrayed on TV. I wondered, "I must look like a real lowlife to this interviewer if she feels that way about me."

Once hired for the logistics job, my opinion gradually changed. I next thought that salespeople simply informed medical professional about the availability of various products. I thought that product selection would be made on the basis of sound clinical research. I pictured doctors sitting around in their lounges reading articles about medical products. I concluded that the salesperson's job must be terribly easy.

I realized I was wrong when I witnessed a young college graduate being interviewed for a sales job by a senior vice president. "Why do you want to sell for us?" asked the VP. "Because your products sell themselves," the candidate responded. "If that's true," retorted the VP, "then why would I need you?"

No smart company pays a person a lot of money to do an easy job.

I spent more time with our salespeople and came to realize the role they had in bringing product information to the doctors. At this time, I decided to take a sales job. I thought I would be spending my time in the lounges with my friends, the doctors, talking about the products.

My first year in sales was an eye-opener. Product decisions were rarely made by doctors. Nurses and purchasing agents were my customers. More surprising was their selection process. While I always believed that I had the best products, my customers rarely bought based on quality alone. My faulty impressions caused me to make many mistakes. Most of these impressions would have been corrected had I read this book.

I have watched Chad Ellis sell for more than ten years. He has a clearer view of the realities of his job than anyone I know. What is more, he possesses a unique ability to express his vision in a way that is understandable.

Medical sales is demanding, competitive, and challenging. If you are reading this book because it looks easy to you, that is only because you have seen people who work hard to make it look easy. Don't forget, Hank Aaron made hitting home runs look easy, too!

Medical sales is rewarding both financially and emotionally. Personal incomes in this field are above average. However, the real payoff comes in the knowledge that you are helping people.

Salespeople have played an important part in the progress of the U.S. health care system over the past 100 years. While they are not more important than nurses, doctors, researchers, and administrators, they are very often the catalysts for change. Medical professionals hate change; it is the sales professional who helps them make change happen.

Our health care system is undergoing rapid changes. The insurance companies and government agencies that pay health care bills are convinced that there is too much waste in the system. This is resulting in drastic changes in the way we sell to our customers. Other changes in the age of the population, technology, and in treatment venue (all detailed beautifully in Chapter 5) are creating an atmosphere of chaos in our industry.

"In chaos is opportunity," one of the leaders in our industry recently said. The simple message here is that you are not going to get ahead by playing it safe. The U.S. population will insist we maintain a high quality health care system. Nevertheless, the pressure to change will realign the way that quality is delivered. When that happens new opportunities will emerge.

What this book offers is a dose of reality. It honestly reflects the future of our industry. It is neither too gloomy nor is it too bright. Anyone who wants to sell to the medical market should read this book. It gives a picture of what the job is like as well as information on how to get the job. Equally, anyone who sells in this marketplace should carry multiple copies of this book. Give a copy to the many customers you encounter who think they want to get into the sales side because it seems like easy work.

As Chad Ellis points out, salespeople are dreamers. This book will not destroy your dream. It will cast it in a new light and give you a practical approach to realizing that dream.

Kevin Whelan
Marketing Manager
Hill-Rom Long Term Care

DEDICATION

This book is dedicated to my wife and life partner, Joyce, who through incredible strength of heart and mind has always demonstrated to me the true meaning of self sacrifice. Grow old with me!

CHAPTER 1

MEDICAL SALES: IS IT FOR ME?

> Nobody dast blame this man.... For a salesman, there is no rock bottom to the life. He don't put a bolt to a nut, he don't tell you the law or give you medicine. He's a man way out there in the blue, riding on a smile and a shoeshine. And when they start not smiling back—that's an earthquake. And then you get yourself a couple of spots on your hat, and you're finished. Nobody dast blame this man. A salesman is got to dream, boy. It comes with the territory.
>
> Charley, in *Death of a Salesman,* "Requiem."

Sellers are dreamers according to Arthur Miller's character; and dreamers, though never absolutely sure of their calling in life, are supremely confident in their own potential and future success. Salespeople are always wondering if another company might pay more for their skills, or if another product might be the wave of the future. Those in real estate wonder if they might "make it big" selling securities. The chemical company representative ponders over the financial possibilities offered by the insurance industry. The vicious circle goes on with dreamers always searching for greener pastures.

The primary purpose of this book is to provide sales dreamers with accurate information to help clarify and focus their understanding of one of those green pastures—medical sales. When armed with a touch of reality, dreamers become opportunists, and certainly the field of medical sales offers rewarding career opportunities. Like any career, however, medical sales has both positive and negative aspects that must be reviewed before a career decision is made. Some of the advantages of a career in medical sales are discussed below.

ADVANTAGES OF A MEDICAL SALES CAREER

Above Average Income

Salespeople in general are compensated more than their company counterparts in areas such as manufacturing or distribution. The Bureau of Labor Statistics reported that the median earnings of manufacturers and wholesale sales representatives were $32,000 in 1992. Medical sales representatives' earnings start at 20 to 40 percent higher than earnings in other sales categories. According to Ralph Steeber, president of Medsearch and a certified personnel consultant, medical sales positions typically start with first-year income packages ranging between $39,000 and $46,000, plus a company automobile and a full expense account.

Although many medical sales incomes have come down in the last few years because of increasing market pressures, a medical sales career still offers sales professionals the opportunity to achieve annual incomes exceeding those in many other professions. With smart planning and hard work, a low six-figure income is possible for many medical sales professionals.

Professional Education and Training

Medical companies are known for the amount of professional education and training provided to their sales employees. Medical professionals such as doctors, nurses, and administrators will not tolerate salespeople who "shoot from the hip" and know little about the products and their intended uses. Medical companies are fully aware that successful salespeople first must be well trained.

Initial training relative to customer needs, market environment, and product performance may last as long as one year before the company begins giving the representative specific sales objectives to reach. The training is usually a mix of headquarters classroom teaching, experienced sales rep mentoring, sales manager coaching, and private studying. The investment that companies make in a new rep's education is substantial since many companies have full-time training departments and are paying rep's salaries during that period before they become productive in selling new business.

They are looking for candidates who can demonstrate good study skills and comprehensive learning.

Training programs are very similar to college course work, and the representatives may be required to pass knowledge and skill tests before actually "selling" to their customers. May medical reps have even said that they will never leave their jobs because they do not want to go through training again with another company! The training period is intense and the expectations are high, but training is essential to long-term success. When interviewing with a company, it is important to know what the training is like and what expectations exist during the training period.

Long-Term Customer Base

Building trust is a must for any salesperson. The shorter the sales cycle, the more difficult trust-building becomes, since fewer customer contacts are made. Because of long sales cycles, most medical sales positions offer the opportunity to develop trust over an extended period of time through many customer contacts. Very little of the medical sales business involves the cold calling or one-time selling that exists in door-to-door or automobile sales, for example. Even capital equipment, which may be bought only once during a decade, requires a long-term record of customer contact.

The end result for the medical sales representative is that many customers also become very close partners in the business of providing health care. As a district sales manager once said, "We're just riding around visiting with our friends." Becoming a business partner (and friend) with the customer is a common expectation, and the customer wants to do business with a company and sales associate who knows everything about his or her challenges and needs. Health care providers are consistently turning to salespeople for help in managing their product needs, and the relationship-building that must take place is a wonderful opportunity for the sales rep to practice the art of managing products and people together.

Another factor that contributes to building a long sales cycle and, therefore, greater job security in medical sales is the aging population in the United States. The population aged eighty-five and over will grow about four times as fast as the total population between now and the year 2005. According to the U.S. Department of Labor, this will result in an increasing demand for health services. Health services also will continue to be one of the fastest growing industries in the economy with overall employment in the sector increasing from 9.6 to 13.8 million. Continued development of high technology health care devices along with the growth in health care services translates to a long-term need for medical sales professionals.

Professional Relationships

Generally, the primary decision makers for medical products are college-educated health care professionals. Typical customers are specialty physicians, department directors, nursing managers, office managers, facility administrators, financial officers, and committees made up of representatives from each of these groups. These management personnel usually will have a technical, nursing, or medical degree with additional training in health care administration. MBAs and MHAs are also becoming more and more popular among health care managers.

The working environment for medical salespeople is characterized by technological change, constant learning, and a spirit of humanitarianism. The sole purpose of medical practice is to help people, and although the ultimate purpose of the medical sales representative is to help a company make a profit, a rep also helps people help people. Building business relationships with health care providers can provide a sense of accomplishing company financial objectives while helping to improve the quality of life for patients. Knowing that a product is helping a medical professional provide quality care can provide a great deal of job satisfaction.

REQUIREMENTS AND CONSIDERATIONS

In addition to the benefits that come from a career in medical sales, consider also the requirements that deserve careful consideration before making the final decision to enter this field.

Commitment

Forty-hour weeks are nonexistent in this field. Be prepared to consistently log sixty or more hours per week as a
medical sales representative. Electronic media have made it
much simpler for salespeople to communicate and also have
made it possible for them to make many more contacts
during the day. With e-mail, voice mail, computers, cellular
phones, pagers, telephones, and fax machines available
around the clock, there are many ways to work with customers that were not available just a few years ago. More
customer contact also means more preparation, more presentations, and more follow-up.

The commitment required to meet customer needs and
expectations means that time for personal hobbies and rec-
reation is greatly diminished. Although customers may
leave work at 3:00 P.M., the sales rep's job is far from over as
work hours often run from 6:00 A.M. to 8:00 P.M. or later. The
rewards are great but the energy and time commitment necessary for success are also great.

Market Pressures

HOME HEALTH SERVICES

Many changes are happening in the health care marketplace that have and will continue to challenge medical sales
representatives. One change that affects where reps do

business is the trend toward home health services. Home health care is the second-fastest growing industry in the economy. Interestingly, hospitals are growing more slowly than any other health service industry despite being the largest sector within health care. This means that companies must figure out how to get their products into the home health market for use on patients who would have been treated in a hospital in the past.

BUYOUTS AND MERGERS

A second challenge for sales personnel in today's medical market is the ongoing process of medical company buyouts and mergers. This has both short-term and long-term effects. Short-term, it means that downsizing of sales forces is an immediate possibility whenever a buyout or merger occurs. Long-term, it means that larger companies emerge with more negotiating power than their smaller competitors. Many medical product companies have so many divergent businesses that they can bundle them together in package deals. Reps working for smaller companies may actually have a better product and/or a better price but not be given business opportunities by potential customers. This happens because the customer cannot afford to have prices go up on several product lines from the bigger company if they decide to buy one product line from the small competitor.

Making a career decision to work for a specific medical company should be based as much on knowledge of the competition as the company being considered. Most product categories have anywhere from two to five major national competitors and often face additional regional competitors as well. Understanding the type of products a company sells and the competing products is a must for future medical representatives.

DIFFERENT PRODUCTS HAVE DIFFERENT SALES NEEDS

A third challenge in today's market is the simple fact that certain types of products have little need for salespeople. A company that sells only Band-Aids to hospitals for example, will probably not have its own sales force because Band-Aids are considered a low-technology product bought and sold primarily on price. Band-Aids can be bought by nonnursing purchasing managers over the telephone without a need for any technical assistance from a salesperson. Many health care products have fallen into this same "commodity" product category over the years, and the more common a product is, the less need there is for an outside representative.

Health care products can be classified into one of three product categories: commodity, proprietary, or new technology. As previously mentioned, *commodity products* are products that are almost identically made by various manufacturers. For example, pillowcases for hospitals and nursing homes are manufactured and sold by several companies with little difference in their products. The most important criterion in this product category is price, since competing products are so similar. Going to work for a company that sells only commodity products probably means that the income potential is lower than it is in other health care sectors, because profit margins tend to be very low.

Proprietary products are those that perform the same job functions as competing products but go about it in a different way. Sales reps for proprietary-type products are needed because customers must be convinced that the "different" way of doing the same thing is the better way. For example, two companies may be competing for a customer's face-mask business with completely different face masks. Both products may perform the job of filtering airborne contaminants, but if one of the masks can be put on with one hand and the other mask takes two, the sales rep may be able to build a case for the "one hand" mask based on convenience or time savings. Typically, proprietary products will have a patent on product design or composition so that competitors cannot simply copy the better product and turn the product into a commodity item. It is always good to know what patent protection might stand behind a company's products.

The final type of product is the *new technology product*. New technology products introduce a new medical practice altogether. When lasers first began to be used for health care applications, new medical methods and procedures began being used for the very first time. Laparoscopic instruments are another great example of a new technology product because they allowed surgeons to perform surgical procedures in a new way that would greatly benefit their patients. Companies selling new technology products will always need salespeople because customers must be taught the new practices after they have seen or experienced the corresponding benefits that the product offers. Generally, the income level generated from selling these products is the highest of the three, and a working knowledge of the company's products and competition will help tremendously in identifying those companies that have the most to offer in terms of both income and job security.

SUMMARY

The field of medical sales is a wonderful place to dream. It offers the opportunity of a fantastic income while working with intelligent, caring people. Medical sales careers are characterized by professional growth through constant education and training while also providing the chance to develop business relationships into long-term friendships. The career is a consuming, challenging one, but one that has financial, professional, and personal rewards. Theodore Roosevelt once said, "Far and away the best prize that life offers is the chance to work hard at work worth doing." Ultimately, a career in medical sales is just that.

CHAPTER 2

PREPARING FOR A CAREER IN MEDICAL SALES

> The life-fate of the modern individual depends not only upon the family into which he was born or which he enters by marriage, but increasingly upon the corporation in which he spends the most alert hours of his best years.
>
> C. Wright Mills, U.S. sociologist

Even though employees do not spend their entire careers with one company the way they did when Mills wrote *The Power Elite* in 1956, selecting an industry or type of business to specialize in has the same "life-fate" effect. After making the decision that medical sales is a career worthy of such commitment, the next step is to develop an understanding of what skills are necessary to compete in the medical sales job market.

A career in medical sales is a Renaissance career. Selling in this field requires broad intellectual interests and individual accomplishments in both the arts and the sciences. The job requires calling on surgeons and janitors, CEOs and housekeepers, nurse managers and office secretaries. It requires the ability to speak to groups of one hundred or solve conflicts with just one. Successful medical sales professionals are of necessity paragons of well-roundedness.

The skills required by medical companies for job candidates are numerous, and the candidate must be able to show expertise in each of them. While reviewing the following criteria, make a list of activities that would demonstrate your proficiency in each area. Here is the list:

NECESSARY SKILLS

What Do Employers Want?

- Problem Solving
- Priority Setting
- Listening
- Public Speaking
- Conflict Resolution

- Achievement
- Organizational
- Persuasion
- Interpersonal

PROBLEM-SOLVING SKILLS

Employers want to see "grace under fire." The medical product area is unique in that having a product available and using it correctly can literally mean the difference in life or death for a patient. How a rep reacts to a back-ordered product or one that is used incorrectly can also have legal implications for the company represented. Problem solving can range from simply figuring out how to get an appointment with a key decision maker to managing the complex implementation of a new product at several institutions simultaneously. To be successful, reps must view problems as opportunities to demonstrate their personal worth to both customer and employer!

PRIORITY-SETTING SKILLS

Most medical reps have several products to represent and many different people or departments on which to call. This requires a great deal of priority setting. Priorities must be set based upon product availability, customer interest, dollar volume potential, profit margins, territory geography, competitive activity, and so forth. Although it may be easier to sell one specific product, a company's sales objectives may require reps to push other products that are actually more difficult to sell. The temptation to spend all of one's time on the easy-to-sell product may be great, but companies want reps who understand their priorities and who set their individual choices accordingly.

LISTENING SKILLS

When asked why he wanted to go into sales, one young candidate replied, "Because I love talking to people." Wrong answer! If he had said, "Because I love listening to people," he may have had a shot at the job. Dean Rusk, a U.S. politician once wrote, "One of the best ways to persuade others is with your ears—by listening to them." How true. In a field where technical information is critical, active listening skills are a must. Reps are obviously required to understand a customer's general needs, such as reducing costs or improving the quality of care, but good listening skills are also essential in this field in order to make sure the right product is being used and the right procedures are being followed. There is a great deal of detail work involved in this field, and managing those details begins with effective listening.

PUBLIC SPEAKING SKILLS

Many sales presentations in today's market are given to product standardization committees, purchasing groups, or hospital alliances that are comprised of department heads from several hospitals. Public speaking skills are an essential tool in the art of selling. As Emerson said, "Speech is power: speech is to persuade, to convert, to compel." Formal presentations must be precisely orchestrated in order to use each allotted minute for the purpose of closing the sale. With more and more product decisions being made by group consensus, strong public speaking ability is becoming increasingly more important in medical sales.

CONFLICT-RESOLUTION SKILLS

Most products in the health care field will have multiple users at one site. Inevitably, one user will want to use the old product and another user will want the new product. Much of the representative's time and effort will be spent in managing through the conflicts that arise through this preference war. There is always old school *vs.* new school argumentation going on within every medical discipline, and although it may not even be related to product use, the end result is that one faction will not like a product simply because the other faction does. As is normally the case, solving these conflicts demands taking on a "parental" role. Pettiness, avarice, greed, and jealousy are alive and well in the health care profession, and the resulting conflicts must be managed by salespeople if they begin to jeopardize the sale.

ACHIEVEMENT/GOAL-SETTING SKILLS

This may be the most important quality that companies look for in a medical representative. Many companies will hire only individuals who can document that they have been at the top of their fields. Companies want reps who have experienced success in achieving specific objectives, both in their personal and professional lives. In addition to documented achievements, companies look for what thought processes and what activities were used in order to bring the alleged success about. Meeting objectives that have been set by an employer or educator are impressive, but managers always seem to be most impressed by difficult goals that were both set and achieved by the achiever.

ORGANIZATIONAL SKILLS

Managing a sales territory is much like having your own business in that the rep is responsible for everything that takes place in the territory. Strong organizational skills are needed to manage product samples, distributor relations, product literature, activity reports, sales forecasting, daily sales calls, and so forth. Companies look for individuals who can demonstrate their ability to handle many tasks simultaneously. Considering the proprietary nature of sales, representatives must wear many different hats, and organizational skills are key in fulfilling various roles.

PERSUASION SKILLS

Individuals who have no previous sales experience always seem to have difficulty breaking into medical sales. However, those who can demonstrate an ability to persuade others into a course of action will get an opportunity regardless of whether they have prior sales experience. Persuasion is

what the sales industry is all about. One of the great plea-
sures of life is to observe an individual or group pursuing a
course of action that you have suggested, and your success
in medical sales is proportional to this skill area more than
any other.

INTERPERSONAL SKILLS

Most of the skills listed in this chapter are rooted in this
last area of interpersonal skills. Problem solving, listening,
conflict resolution, and persuading all take place one-on-one
with the customer. Interestingly, however, the largest percentage of a rep's time is spent alone, while driving, planning, practicing, calculating, and so forth. The quality of
time spent face-to-face with customers represents the effort
and preparation put in by the sales rep while alone, and in
order to maximize face time with a customer, interpersonal
communication must be both precise and motivational.

The sales process can be broken down into the two basic
areas of planning and persuading. Reps are always either
planning to sell or attempting to close the sale. Planning is
the mediation phase and persuading is the motivation phase.
*Intra*personal skills lay the foundation for the sale, but
strong *inter*personal skills are required in order to make sure
that action is actually taken after the exchange of ideas
occurs with a customer.

An assertive approach works best in this field, assertive being defined as "aggressiveness with finesse." Many of the customers called on by medical sales reps are more educated and higher paid than are the reps. Therefore, the customer's mindset is one that cannot be sold by intimidation or heavy-handed sales tactics. Realizing the role ego plays in the health care profession and responding to it with respect and professionalism are the key interpersonal skills employers look for. Companies want individuals whose interpersonal skills are strong enough to deliver results.

CHAPTER 3

ON THE JOB

> The greatest analgesic, soporific, stimulant, tranquil-
> izer, narcotic, and to some extent even antibiotic—in
> short, the closest thing to a genuine panacea—known
> to medical science is work.
>
> Thomas Szasz

Work can bring both pleasure and pain, fun and failure. The best way to maximize the opportunities for pleasure and fun is to make sure that the career being sought requires activities you enjoy. Generally, salespeople in all industries are responsible for developing customer interest in a company's products and ensuring that any client questions or concerns are handled appropriately. Such a job description usually leads most people to say, "Anybody could do that!" Indeed, many try, yet few can professionally execute all of the job activities required of a successful medical sales representative.

Selling for a company or corporation is the next best thing to owning a business (some reps even suggest it is *better* than owning a business!). The employee is in charge of everything that goes on in the territory, but the fiscal responsibility rests solely on the shoulders of the employer. That might be the "panacea" that Szasz was describing. Medical sales can be an entrepreneur's delight, but many hats must be worn during the course of managing a sales territory.

The obvious expectation for a sales employee is to meet company-set performance objectives. The primary purpose of this chapter, however, is to highlight the key job activities that are performed in order to bring about the achievement of specific sales objectives and quotas.

ACTIVITIES

What Do Employers Expect?

- Product Presentations
- Concept Presentations
- Territory Management
- Distributor Management
- OEM Management
- In-services/Customer Training
- Phone Work
- Administration

PRODUCT PRESENTATIONS

Most medical companies sell hundreds or even thousands of different products. This means that salespeople must constantly study product technical data in order to fully acquaint themselves with product codes, performance, features, benefits, pricing, packaging, and so forth. Medical reps must be able to efficiently import key product information to customers who are limited in the amount of time they have available to listen to product presentations. Health care professionals do want new product information when their jobs can be made easier, safer, or more cost effective, but they need complete information *quickly.*

Many positions, such as pharmaceutical positions, serve as "teachers" to their customers. Reps must know as much or more about the product and the disease it was designed to treat than the practitioner doing the treating. Accuracy in product presentation is critical in the health care business.

Product presentation is often required both before and after the sale. *Before the sale* presentations are geared toward detailing the features and benefits of a specific product for the purpose of getting an order. *After the sale* presentations are designed to help the clinician use the product effectively. Although most product presentations occur in a nonpractice environment, some sales positions will require the ability to talk a practitioner through the steps of product use during situations involving direct patient care.

Because medical representatives must be so concise in their product presentations, many companies are more concerned with finding reps who possess an excellent command of the English language than they are in hiring those with science backgrounds similar to their clients. Language skills are paramount to effectively presenting products to the customer. Each presentation must have clarity, and more importantly, it must have a goal.

CONCEPT PRESENTATIONS

Although the skills used when presenting a product or a concept may be very similar, concept presentations require the ability to demonstrate abstract ideas. For example, Company X may have three major product lines (such as gloves, sutures, and cauteries) with each line consisting of several product codes that may vary in size, materials, and strengths. Assuming that Company X's brands are second in market share to three different companies that sell only one line of product each (Company A has the #1 glove line, Company B has the #1 suture line, and Company C has the #1 cautery line), Company X must now take an ideational approach toward potential customers. In this case, the approach might conceptualize the potential cost savings achieved by doing business with one company instead of three. Through vendor reduction, Company X could help the customer reduce purchase orders, reduce the number of reps to work with, streamline inventories, and so forth. The company would certainly provide an acceptable product, but in order to get the business it would have to sell the benefits of a *concept,* such as vendor reduction, instead of a specific product.

As lowering supply costs becomes more important to health care facilities, product advantages become less important in the mind of the customer. Conceptually presenting what the product can accomplish is much more critical than simply demonstrating the features and benefits of a product. When presenting a product, the customer can easily see it. When presenting an idea, the customer can see only the portrait a representative is able to paint with his or her words.

TERRITORY MANAGEMENT

Territory management is the science of putting company sales objectives into place within the geographical confines of an individual sales territory. This begins by analyzing what opportunities exist within the territory. The analysis is based in part on knowledge of competing products, customer satisfaction, and product volume potential. A representative may, for instance, have to decide that it is a better sales choice to spend time with a customer who is completely satisfied with a competing product than it is to spend time with a customer who is dissatisfied with the same prod-

RENNER LEARNING RESOURCE CENTER
ELGIN COMMUNITY COLLEGE
ELGIN, ILLINOIS 60123

uct, if converting the satisfied customer represents enough business potential to meet the required sales objectives for a much longer period of time.

Territory management is essentially an exercise in setting priorities. For example, reps must:

- decide how to divide their time between current and potential customers
- determine how to route their travel to maximize time in front of clients
- develop and manage customer databases and files to ensure that decisions are based on accurate information
- manage customer contracts
- forecast sales for manufacturing purposes
- prepare accurate expense and activity reports

When interviewing with a medical company, it is important to review what tools are provided to reps for the express purpose of territory management.

DISTRIBUTOR MANAGEMENT

Few medical product companies sell directly to the customer. Most health care facilities will utilize the distribution services offered by companies that specialize in distribution. Once a hospital, clinic, or center decides on a specific product, they ask their distributor to order the product into the distributor's warehouse. The health care center will then order the product from the distributor when it is needed, thus the term *just-in-time* inventory.

The distribution of products through a distributor offers many benefits to both the end user and the manufacturer. However, additional responsibilities for the manufacturer/ representative grow out of this relationship. The manufacturer/rep must help manage the introduction of new products, work with distributor sales representatives to close new business, assist in determining proper inventory levels, confirm proper filing of contracts and rebates, and provide up-to-date product information to a distributor's customer service reps. Even though a manufacturer targets and closes new business at the end user level, the distributor becomes the legal customer of the manufacturer because it is the distributor who actually buys the product. In effect, medical companies have two customers: the end user and the distributor who services the end user. Meeting the needs of both is critical for sales growth in today's market.

OEM MANAGEMENT

There can at times be one additional customer in the sales process: the original equipment manufacturer (see Chapter 4). This customer is a company that buys products from several manufacturers and then repackages all of the products into one new package. The advantage for the end user is that he or she has all of the products needed for a specific patient procedure and does not have to deal with the packaging waste and labor involved in managing all of the items individually. OEMs are selling a service, and they utilize an entire sales force just like manufacturers or distributors. OEM reps can also exert their influence at the account level as to which products go in to their repackaged product.

When end users decide to utilize OEM companies, the medical product rep must then manage sales through three steps. The end user makes the product decision, informs the OEM company what products they want repackaged, and then advises the distributor of their inventory needs. The chain can get very complicated, and helping manage business growth with both distributor and OEM supplier is an integral part of a manufacturer rep's job.

IN-SERVICES/CUSTOMER TRAINING

The slightest change in product use can result in what end users see as dramatic change in their practices. Additionally, many practitioners not involved in the actual selection of a product assume that all new products are cheaper, less effective substitutes for the incumbent product. Therefore sales personnel must first make sure that new customers are aware of any practice changes that the new product may bring about, and then they must also present it in a way that romances the product as a clinical upgrade.

In-services are short educational periods designed to inform health care staffers of personnel, policy, product, or practice changes. Health care facilities expect medical sales reps to provide this service whenever product training is necessary. In-services are usually completed before a new product goes into use, and this is a great time for salespeople to solidify the sale. Many facilities will enter into product evaluation phases before a final decision is made, and the in-service sets the tone for that evaluation. Reps are provided the opportunity to discuss the technical and functional aspects of products during in-service periods, and a successful in-service is usually proportionate to creativity in presenting the material and refreshments provided to the staff.

PHONE WORK

Customers in the health care field will rarely see salespeople unless an appointment has been pre-arranged or a standing appointment is agreed upon. This means that a lot time is spent daily on the telephone trying to make those appointments with elusive decision makers. Evening hours are spent calling distributor and OEM reps to follow up on end user requests. Most companies and customers do have voice mail systems to ease the challenge of staying in touch, but trying to make customer appointments over voice mail is still too impersonal for initial contacts.

Make a note to find out who pays for the phone bills. It is very easy to run up monthly charges in the range of $400–$500, and while cellular phones certainly make the job easier, they are expensive. Telephone use can be both costly and frustrating, but telephone contact is the birthplace of every good sales call.

ADMINISTRATION

Administration—another word for paperwork, and in the electronic age, computerwork! Employer's generally require that representatives provide three basic kinds of reports: activity, expense, and forecast reports. Though not the most exciting activity around, reporting is absolutely necessary in order to precisely deploy the sales force, efficiently manage sales expense budgets, and accurately forecast production schedules to ensure adequate product supply.

Activity reports may include daily, weekly, and/or monthly reports that describe who the rep has called on, what products or concepts were presented, and what results were obtained. Pharmaceutical companies that require regularly scheduled physician contacts, for example, will develop complex databases from activity reports in order to provide their reps with territory managements tools. These tools are designed to remind reps when they last called on a customer, what was discussed during the appointment, what product usage information was given, and when they need to make another call. Activity reports are also used by senior management to assist in the development of a sales force strategy and in performance reviews for individual reps.

Expense reports must be completed and accurate because they are used to support gross income adjustments and tax advantages for the company. Expenses are usually handled either by allowing reps to write themselves a reimbursement check up to an approved level, by paying the expenses back in arrears, or by charging expenses directly to the company. The second method could mean that a rep has personally paid for several weeks worth of expenses before any compensatory payment has been made. Reps generally prefer the first or last method.

Forecasting is the process of determining how much product a company should manufacture over a given time period. It is an inexact science based on historical product usage and estimated new business. Forecasting reports are very critical for both the company and the customer. If a company builds up too much inventory, the company suffers due to the costs of carrying excess product. However, if too little product is made and back orders result, customers suffer because they are forced to spend time finding an alternate supplier or, in extreme cases, to cancel patient procedures. Some companies have specific personnel in charge of this process so that the forecasting responsibility for sales reps is minimized, but forecasting is an essential job activity.

SUMMARY

The skills and activities required of a medical sales representative indicate the need for generalists rather than specialists. Broad knowledge of many fields is much more important than infinite knowledge in one subject area. The career is exciting because the required diversity in knowledge and ability means that the environment is constantly changing, and constant change dictates constant personal and professional growth.

CHAPTER 4

THE SEVEN TYPES
OF MEDICAL COMPANIES

To business that we love we rise betime,
And go to't with delight.

William Shakespeare

Medical companies offer great variety to the professional salesperson because of the many types of companies that exist. Rather than viewing this sales field as a single "category" of sales, it is best perceived as a diverse industry consisting of several distinct enterprises. There are no fewer than seven classes of medical companies with each being identified by unique differences in products and services. Each type of company is briefly reviewed to give the reader a basic understanding of the unique business environment in which the companies operate.

CAPITAL EQUIPMENT COMPANIES

Capital equipment companies manufacture products that represent a large capital investment by a medical facility.

These are products such as lasers, sterilizers, beds, or operating room lights that can range in cost from several hundred to several million dollars. Although an individual institution's monetary qualifications for capital equipment may vary, financial officers will ordinarily identify capital equipment as any product priced on a per unit basis at $1,000 or greater. When planning to purchase capital equipment, medical institutions customarily write purchase specifications and seek competitive bids.

For the most part, capital equipment companies employ a small number of sales representatives to handle large geographic territories. Many of the sales opportunities are one-time opportunities, because the products sold may have a longer life than the rep's career will last. Unit sales for these companies are usually low, but unit cost and profit are correspondingly high.

Sales Highlight

Income opportunity in capital equipment sales is the highest of all types with annual incomes into the highly sought after six-figure area. However, it can be a feast or famine business as many companies pay based on a straight commission. The challenges and rewards are accordingly high.

MEDICAL/SURGICAL COMPANIES

Medical/surgical (Med/Surg) companies specialize in single-use or low-cost-per-unit reusable products. These products, which must be regularly replenished, range from Band-Aids and gauze sponges to sutures and surgical drapes. Although the unit prices of these products are low (at times less than $1.00), their high volume can often push them to the highest percentage of a hospital's supply budget. For example, a hospital performing 10,000 surgical procedures per year (typical for a 350–400 bed hospital), may spend as much as $400,000 to $500,000 annually on sutures and wound closure products.

Hospitals, surgery centers, and clinics often buy med/surg products through national contracts arranged by group purchasing organizations (see additional GPO discussion in Chapter 5). As such, a sales representative may become more of a contract implementation specialist than a sales professional. It is extremely important to know if the company you are considering has GPO contracts and whether the products can be sold without them. Also consider whether the company will actually see you as a "service" or "sales" person. It could make a difference in the long-term income opportunities.

Sales Highlight

Medical/surgical companies have sales forces that range up to a couple of hundred salespeople. Because of this size, there are usually one to three levels of sales management, which translates into more career development opportunities. If sales management is your long-term career goal, med/surg companies offer plenty of opportunity. Income levels vary greatly in this category, and most companies will pay their representatives a base salary plus an additional bonus or commission tied into overall sales performance.

MANUFACTURER REPRESENTATION FIRMS

Many medical companies are so small that they can not deploy an independent sales force to market their products. The expense is simply too great. As such, companies turn to private firms who represent many manufacturers. The manufacturer representative is essentially a medical mercenary who may work alone or with a small group of other independent reps incorporated as a privately owned firm.

Manufacturer representation (MR) firms have very broad product lines and are constantly adding and deleting products from their offerings. The products represented could be highly specialized one-of-a-kind items, an initial product offering from a foreign manufacturer, or a medically related product from a consumer product company. Versatility is a necessary character trait in this field as new products are the lifeblood of the business. This requires constant training in product knowledge.

Sales Highlight

MR sales is truly the entrepreneurial segment of the market in that a rep's personal financial responsibility is at its greatest. Because MR reps are frequently treated as independent contractors, they usually have to pay for expenses, but they benefit with a salary resulting from an agreed upon percentage of sales with the manufacturer. Because the business is proprietary in nature (as a manufacturing rep, you do not usually report to a "manager"), it is *your* business. If independence is what you are seeking, this may be the avenue to pursue. Keep in mind, though, that the person succeeding in this area usually has years of medical sales experience and has built strong business relationships with an existing customer base. If you are trying to break into the field, you might persuade an existing MR firm to take you on a trial basis, since you would be paid only on closed sales.

ORIGINAL EQUIPMENT MANUFACTURER

Original equipment manufacturer (OEM) companies have grown substantially in the marketplace since the mid-1980s, and they can be broken down into two subgroups. The first and largest OEM companies are known as *custom tray* manufacturers. They buy products from other medical companies and then repackage them in order to better meet a hospital's product needs for specific patient procedures. Since the sales platform is based primarily on the principles of labor and waste reduction, custom tray selling is more conceptual than product related selling.

The second subgroup of OEM companies manufacture private label products for medical/surgical companies that want to sell a specific product without actually making the capital investment to manufacture it. This is similar to a car parts maker who would make the seat cover material to be used in assembling a car. These companies usually have limited sales personnel because their target customers may be one or two other major manufacturers instead of the end user of the product.

Sales Highlight

OEM representatives can make a nice living by developing business in just a few accounts since one large account can represent $1 million or more in annual sales. If you enjoy building long-term relationships, are motivated by problem-solving and cost-reduction challenges, and are extremely organized, you will greatly enjoy this marketplace.

PHARMACEUTICAL COMPANIES

Pharmaceutical companies such as Johnson & Johnson, Merck, and Schering-Plough promote their prescription drug products to physicians and pharmacists through dedicated sales forces. The company representatives detail their products to health care providers for the express purpose of increasing the number of patient prescriptions. This type of selling is indirect because the end user who buys the product actually knows very little about it. Pharmaceutical representatives are educators who solicit the influence of a third party upon end users.

Pharmaceutical companies can have sales personnel numbering into the hundreds, and this sales category provides more employment opportunities than do the other six. Sales training and ongoing professional education must necessarily be outstanding because physicians and other health professionals view reps as a primary source of their pharmaceutical education. Sales performance in this category is somewhat subjective because you do not leave a doctor's office with a physical order, however you do have the opportunity to develop a strong supporter who can be a product proponent for months and years to come.

Sales Highlight

By demonstrating superior product knowledge to customers, pharmaceutical sales representatives can nurture their professional relationships to the point that they are viewed as true consultants or subject matter experts. This is a great sales category for individuals who enjoy the consultant/educator role, and due to the large number of sales position, it also provides more opportunity to break into the medical sales field.

DISTRIBUTION COMPANIES

In order to reduce materials management costs, health care providers (HCP) prefer to buy from the smallest number of companies possible. Therefore, most manufacturers actually sell their products to a distribution company, such as Baxter International or General Medical, which in turn "resells" the product to the end user. This allows the HCP to benefit from "just-in-time" and "stockless" inventory programs offered by distribution companies. Distributor sales representatives are responsible for selling the efficiency of their distribution programs and also play a major role in making sure that the supply chain from manufacturer to end user is never broken.

Distribution companies range in size from national distributors to smaller, regional distributors that may only cover accounts in a few cities. Distributors may focus on providing every product known to health care or, in the case of specialty distributors, sell products related to only one medical specialty such as neurosurgery. Some companies may have sales divisions. For example, one division may be selling to the hospital market and another division may sell only to the physician market. Territories for the national companies are small, and profits are made through high volume and inventory turns, not high-profit margins. Group purchasing organizations have drastically driven down distributor profit margins over the last fifteen years. This means that efficiency, organization, attention to detail, and great communication skills are vital for the success of a distributor sales rep and the company represented.

Sales Highlight

The relationships built by distributor representatives are so strong that the end user eventually begins to see the rep as part of the end user institution. The reps can have a lot of power in product evaluation and selection because they are in the facility on a frequent basis (sometimes as much as daily) and develop a great understanding of the customer's needs. Individuals who enjoy being "part of the family" make successful distributor reps.

CONSUMER PRODUCT OVER-THE-COUNTER COMPANIES

Pharmaceutical, medical/surgical, and consumer product companies also manufacture nonprescription consumer products with a medical indication. Pepto-Bismol, made by Procter & Gamble, and Visine, by Pfizer, are good examples of such products. Many of these companies have salespeople who specialize in promoting these products through both traditional merchandising efforts and direct marketing to physician specialties.

This medical sales segment is unique in that the over-the-counter (OTC) rep can be employed by a small division of a Fortune 500 company. It is like working for a start-up com-

pany in that there is lots of room for sales imagination and
flexibility, but you also have the security of being backed by
a financially strong corporation. Some of these companies
also employ flex-time employees who work twenty-five to
thirty hours per week, so this is a great area for individuals
who do not really want full-time work or need the personal
benefits associated with a full-time position.

Sales Highlight

Much like the pharmaceutical sales category, representatives of OTC companies serve as educators or professional
communicators. Job performance is usually activity related
(i.e., a rep must call on seven rheumatologists a day), and
task-oriented individuals will enjoy this environment.

SUMMARY OF COMPANIES

These seven types of companies have different character-
istics and sales approaches. It is important when considering a company to understand the differences and how they
might impact a career decision. The differences become
advantages or disadvantages only when applied to individual circumstances. For example, capital equipment companies require lots of travel because the territories are usually
very large. A sales representative with a family might frame
the situation as undesirable, while a single person may view
high travel requirements as a wonderful opportunity to visit

new locations. Only you can decide which would be best for you.

JOB CRITERIA

In the following chart, eleven criteria are presented for consideration when deciding which type of company would best fit one's ideal employer profile. The criteria are: income, travel, benefits, expenses, training, previous experience, paperwork load, advancement opportunity, performance measurement, orientation, and structure. A brief discussion of each requirement, based on anecdotal evidence and professional experience, follows:

TYPE OF COMPANY							
Job Criteria	*Capital Equip.*	*Med/Surg*	*M.R. Firm*	*O.E.M.*	*Pharma.*	*Distrib.*	*CP/OTC*
Income (in $1,000s)	$100–200	$50–100	$60–80	$40–75	$40–60	$30–60	$30–60
Travel	80%	20%	40%	10%	10%	0%	10%
Benefits	Above Avg.	Above Avg.	Below Avg.	Avg.	Above Avg.	Avg.	Avg.
Expenses	Company	Company	Personal	Personal	Company	Personal	Company
Training	Moderate	Lengthy	Abbreviated	Moderate	Lengthy	Abbreviated	Moderate
Prev. Experience	Med Sales	Sales	Medical	Medical	Success	Success	Success
Paperwork (Hrs/Day)	1	1	2	4	1	4	1
Advancement Opportunity	Low	High	Low	Moderate	High	Low	Moderate
Performance Measurement	Objective	Objective	Objective	Objective	Subjective	Subjective	Subjective
Orientation	Sales	S&S	Sales	S&S	S&S	Service	S&S
Structure	Horizontal	Vertical	Horizontal	Horizontal	Vertical	Horiz/Vert	Vertical

Income

Income levels vary proportionately to performance orientation. If the sales objective is production oriented in the sense that the company pays the rep only when a product is sold, income is usually higher than when the company pays a salary for activity-oriented performance, which may not result in an immediate product purchase. Capital equipment companys' payouts are the highest, and along with MR firms, usually pay based on straight commission. The remaining five categories base pay on some combination of salary and bonus or commission.

Salary plus bonus or commission pay plans need to be fully understood before committing to a sales position. Higher base salaries do not necessarily mean higher pay because usually the higher pay positions end up paying much more in commissions than in base pay. By asking the company for an example of an average rep's payout for the previous year, one can see the percentage of salary and commission that makes up the total compensation. Generally, the companies with lower base salaries offer higher overall income potential, and this is usually accompanied by higher performance expectations.

Commission plans pay based on products actually sold. The plan could be based on any number of methods, including a percentage of total dollar volume, varying commission amounts based on unit profitability, and payouts that change based on performance versus a predetermined quota. Bonus plans differ slightly from commission plans since bonus programs pay a set amount for the achievement of a specific goal, and commission plans are usually open ended (no maximum cap).

For example, under a bonus plan, a rep may earn a $4,000 bonus at the end of the year if 100 percent of the sales objective is achieved. Under a commission plan, however, a rep may be paid 5 percent of net sales for all products sold up to 100 percent of quota and 8 percent of net for every product sold above quota. Income potential is normally greater in commission plans than in bonus plans, but it is imperative to understand both the company's plan and the territory opportunities before estimating the income potential of a specific position.

Travel

Travel is one of those job requirements that goes hand in hand with sales of any kind. Travel in medical sales can range from practically no overnight travel for the distributor rep who calls on five to ten accounts in one city, to four or five overnights a week for the capital equipment rep who covers the eastern half of the United States. The percentages expressed in the chart are intended as guides to help the reader understand how much of a five-night work week might be spent away from home.

Travel is related to geography and number of accounts. Each company considered as a potential employer should have drawn maps of the territory and a list of accounts in the area to be covered. Deciding how much travel is required before accepting a position is an essential part of reviewing a sales representative opportunity.

Benefits

Benefits provided by a company can be just as important as the income potential, and they deserve careful consideration. For comparison, "average" benefits are defined as medical and dental insurance, a two-week vacation, job-related expenses, a company car, and a retirement/pension plan. In the chart, "below average" is anything less and "above average" is anything more. When calculating the total compensation potential of a job offer, place a monetary value on each benefit offered and on any required personal contributions. A benefit package might include:

- medical insurance
- dental insurance
- vacation
- retirement/pension plan
- life insurance
- disability insurance (long-term and short-term)
- professional education
- college fund
- matching stock purchase program
- 401K program
- child care

- company car
- job-related expenses
- performance-related trips/vacations/prizes

The benefits portion of a compensation package can easily be worth as much as 40 to 50 percent of the monetary part. Careful attention to benefits provides a better understanding of exactly how much a sales position is worth.

Expenses

Most companies pay for overnight travel expenses, car and related costs, secretarial and office expenses, telephone bills, and so forth, that are incurred as a direct result of operating the business. Companies with small territories and those that view their reps as independent contractors often require reps to pay their own expenses. Recognize that a sales territory may incur annual sales expenses nearing the actual pay of the position, so know who pays the bills!

The expense reimbursement method can also have an impact on income. Check to see if a company representative is reimbursed weekly or if the rep has to carry the expenses for several weeks while waiting to be reimbursed. Many companies have a voucher or company check system whereby the rep can receive personal weekly reimbursement. Others simply turn in an expense report that must first be audited and approved before any funds will be issued. There is also a trend today for many companies to use corporate credit cards to reduce the amount of out-of-pocket expenses incurred.

Training

On the chart, training for each of the seven types of companies is described as either abbreviated, moderate, or lengthy. Abbreviated is defined as 0–3 months, moderate is 3–6 months, and lengthy is beyond 6 months. The companies that have a lot of products and require reps to be able to fully demonstrate the functionality of those products have the most lengthy training programs. Training takes place in the home office, at off-site training locations, in the rep's own territory, and in experienced rep territories. Training can be intense and competitive. Companies expect top performance in training and have been known to terminate individuals who did not pass training tests and develop basic job skill requirements.

After initial product training, companies often provide advanced sales training that emphasizes sales skills more than product knowledge. Companies may also conduct regular sales meetings and sales training seminars to further develop their sales forces.

Previous Experience

If you are just getting started in the pursuit of a medical sales position, it is a good idea to understand how your previous work experience will be viewed by a potential employer in this field.

Pharmaceutical companies, distributors, and CP/OTCs are looking for a pattern of success in jobs that have required strong leadership and communication skills. They do not necessarily require sales experience as long as you can document your successes and skills in your previous position.

Medical/surgical companies are looking for individuals with strong sales backgrounds and they demand documentation of sales results. Sales managers want the superstars from other industries who can prove that they have been in the top percentage of salespeople in their field. Medical sales is not a requirement but sales success is a must.

Capital equipment companies, MR firms, and OEMs normally require previous medical or medical sales experience. A primary reason is that these companies want an individual who can build business based on relationships with previous customers in the medical field. Medical professionals such as nurses or purchasing personnel can also transition into selling because they are well acquainted with a company's products through personal use, and they have strong professional relationships with accounts in which they previously worked.

Paperwork

Ah, the bane of a sales rep's existence...paperwork! Unfortunately paperwork is an absolute must in just about any sales position. In the medical field, OEM and distributor reps are mostly heavily involved in the paper pushing experience. Accuracy and timeliness are crucial in order for customers to get the correct products exactly when they need them. If paperwork is on your list of annoying activities, stay away from these two areas. The remaining company types require one to two hours of daily paperwork, which may include placing orders, writing follow-up letters, completing sales activity reports, forecasting, reporting expenses, and requesting product samples.

Advancement Opportunity

Advancement opportunity is tied directly to the size of the company and the sales force... the bigger, the better. The greatest opportunities for reps to move into sales or product management are found in medical/surgical and pharmaceutical companies. In the largest companies, sales reps can move out of sales into marketing, training, distribution, sales administration, sales management, and even research and development. Companies with small numbers of employees simply do not offer many career paths or management opportunities, however, small companies often provide a "family" environment not found elsewhere.

Performance Measurement

Measurement of a sales representative's performance by comparing actual sales versus a given objective is the easiest and most accurate method of gauging productivity. Objective performance measurement allows sales production to speak for itself without making any qualitative assessments about how the numbers were reached. Companies using objective measurement do not place many activity requirements upon their employees, and the politics of which managers like which reps best does not cloud performance evaluations. As long as quotas are met, great flexibility and freedom is given to the individual reps in choosing their own sales methods and approaches; however, there is little patience with reps who consistently miss sales objectives.

Subjective performance measurement is required in the businesses where the sales rep is not directly influencing the product end user to place an order. Measuring performance in this way must be done in large part by a manager's personal observation of the rep or by interviewing the representative's customers for additional feedback. Activity-oriented objectives are also frequently implemented in order to measure the results of an entire sales force. For example, a pharmaceutical company may ask all reps to call on two cardiologists a day for one quarter to promote a new drug. This is an activity that is easily measured, and the company will later determine if the activity was effective by monitoring sales to drug distributors and pharmacies for that specific drug during and immediately after the activity period. An individual's performance is measured by his or her ability to make the two calls per day.

In reality, most companies use a combination of both measurement methods. Recognize, however, that the major difference is that objective-based measurement says, "We want $450,000 in new business, go get it!", and subjective-based measurement says, "We want you to make fifteen calls a day, and we want you to do each one like this...." Both systems work, but a rep may be more comfortable working in one system over the other. Ask for a blank copy of an annual performance review to determine exactly what the company will expect.

Orientation

Sales can be defined as all activity necessary to bring the customer to the point of purchase. Service can be defined as all activity necessary to support the customer's purchase. Distributor companies are almost exclusively service related, while capital equipment manufacturers and MR firms are particularly sales oriented. The remaining company types provide both sales and service to the customer and one often hinges on the other. Service to an account may include product distribution, staff education and in-servicing, ongoing product assessment programs, and provision of external consulting services. Product support and service programs can be a determining factor in closing a sale, and the sales representative must manage these programs before, during, and after the sale as part of daily sales activities. Some companies also provide service personnel (for support of the sales rep and the customer) to monitor and maintain instruments and equipment. Keep in mind that service time takes away from selling time, so if you are interviewing with a company that pays little commission on existing business that requires frequent service calls, your money-making opportunities will be reduced. Examine the existing business and how much service support it requires.

Structure

The final item to consider is the structure of the sales organization. It may be either horizontal or vertical. Companies that have few reps will have a horizontal structure, i.e., they will not have many layers of management. The owners or managers will be on the same level as the sales representatives, and the organizational chart will be flat. This speeds up the decision-making process and also increases the business flexibility that may be needed on a specific account. Horizontal structure does, however, limit advancement opportunities.

Conversely, a vertical sales structure results when large sales organizations have several management levels. This slows down decision making because a decision often must be pushed upward in the organization. Business flexibility also decreases because many decisions are based on policies written for an entire sales force. Vertical structure, however, does provide the greatest number of advancement opportunities and includes a more exact approach to sales activities.

SUMMARY OF CHART

All of the criteria in the chart are meant to provide a starting point into your investigation of a medical sales position. The descriptions of the types of companies are general guidelines and exceptions will be found. Use them as a place to begin your job search recognizing that one's professional satisfaction is contingent upon knowing as much as possible about the industry and position.

CHAPTER 5

TRENDS IN HEALTH
CARE PURCHASING

> It is change, continuing change, inevitable change,
> that is the dominant factor in society today. No sensi-
> ble decision can be made any longer without taking
> into account not only the world as it is, but the world
> as it will be.... This, in turn, means that our states-
> men, our businessmen, our everyman must take on a
> science fictional way of thinking.
>
> Isaac Asimov

It may not be science fiction but purchasing trends in health care have been in a state of rapid change since the early 1980s with the passage of the federal government's Tax Equity and Fiscal Responsibility Act. During the years since the passage of that law, health care facilities have gone through incredible evolution in the way products are bought and managed. These changes have been precipitated largely by the different ways in which patients access and pay for health care.

Three changes in health care delivery are responsible for variation in purchasing habits. The first noteworthy change is that health care providers (HCP) are no longer reimbursed on a fee-for-service system. HCPs have historically totaled up the bill for treating a patient and then passed those charges along to the payer such as an insurance company. The bill was simply a result of every charge in the treatment process being forwarded for payment. If the HCP used a product costing $10 for patient treatment, the HCP was reimbursed. If another HCP used a more expensive product ($20) for the same treatment, they, too, were reimbursed. Under this system, there was no incentive for the HCP to aggressively control costs, and there was more emphasis on product quality than on product price.

CAPITATION

Instead of the fee-for-service system, most health care is now prepaid. This means that a health care plan may be negotiated between provider and payer for a flat fee that is paid before any service is actually rendered. The provider is usually a type of health maintenance organization (HMO) that includes both general practice and specialty physicians. The HMO will provide a complete and comprehensive range of health services to the payer for a fixed amount of money over a specified period of time. The result is that HCPs are actually rewarded for keeping the cost of delivering health care down. This new approach is know as *capitation.*

Capitation can be defined as the relationship between a provider and insurer whereby the provider is paid a fixed amount for each plan member per time period for a defined set of services. The goal of capitation is to decrease cost and maintain lower levels of cost over longer periods of time. This system motivates providers to hold down costs because they can directly profit from their success. Providers have little to no incentive to request more diagnostic tests, hospitalize patients, or refer them to extensively trained specialists. Basically, under this system, providers can achieve better financial results by limiting the utilization of their health care services.

Managed care as described above, has immediate impact on medical supply companies and their sales employees. HCPs are becoming much more aggressive in their negotiations with suppliers because every product price reduction means positive movement in the provider's profits. Although product quality is still important to HCPs they are expecting price concessions from manufacturers in return for long-term business commitments. Long-term contracts do help manufacturers become more effective in production forecasting, and in turn this helps in managing the costs of making and selling products. The ultimate goal of capitation is to drive cost out of every part of the health care system.

On an individual level, the medical sales representative will have to change to more of a partner rather than a traditional product seller. Once reps develop business with a HCP, their performance will be measured by how well they partner with the customer in areas such as appropriate product utilization. Service from reps becomes more important than sales because without service there is no sale. Managed care will demand that salespeople spend more time making sure that customers are using the right product for the right application in order that the customer can meet their financial objectives. Reps who can demonstrate the ability to further drive costs out of their customer's health care delivery system will succeed.

GROUP PURCHASING ORGANIZATIONS

A second change seen in health care today is the change in venue. In the past, most care was provided in a hospital setting. This has dramatically changed due primarily to new medical technologies. Approximately 60 percent of health care is now provided in an outpatient setting, and that shift also means that many health care products that previously had been used in hospitals, are now being used in an outpatient or home health environment. To equal the purchasing power formerly found in hospitals, many outpatient centers and clinics are joining forces with each other and with hospitals as part of group purchasing organizations (GPOs). GPOs have been around for nearly two decades, but they were previously made up of hospitals alone. Now they consist of many types of providers and are also changing their business methods.

There are several group purchasing organizations in the United States with names such as MedEcon, VHA, AmeriNet, Premier, and SCA. These companies solicit members from hospitals, outpatient clinics, and physician groups and charge their members annual membership fees. Their basic purpose is to use membership power to negotiate better contracts with suppliers than the members could manage on their own. GPOs focus their attention on two main issues: contracts and compliance. Each is dependent on the other. Product suppliers want to negotiate contracts and will provide their best pricing to those groups that can bring the highest level of compliance to the contract. GPOs in turn will guarantee their highest levels of commitment to contracts that represent the highest savings to their members.

GPOs affect salespeople in much the same way as managed care in that the service aspect becomes more important than the sales function. Large medical manufacturers usually have a national accounts team that negotiates group contracts, and the individual reps have little influence on that process. The national accounts team is responsible for selling a company's products and services to the GPO. When a company signs a national GPO contract, the sales personnel are responsible for the implementation of the contract, and while there is some selling involved, most rep activities are geared toward proper product selection and use. GPOs want to enhance partnering with suppliers in order to improve contract compliance because this can further reduce product prices on future group agreements.

As you seek a career with a medical company, make sure you know what relationship exists with national and regional GPOs. More specifically, ask what GPOs are represented in the territory you are interviewing for, and determine if the company has a contract with those organizations. If you take a job with a company that has no GPO agreements and your major competitors do have them, you may have a very difficult time making a living. Companies do want GPO agreements, but when they do not get them, they do their best to ruin compliance of contracts awarded to competing companies. GPOs are aware of this, and they are doing a complete job of making sure that there are penalties for noncompliance and financial rewards for compliance. The success of manufacturers in the last half of the decade will be directly determined by their ability to forge new and maintain existing GPO contracts.

Hospitals are branching out on the GPO concept a bit further in that many are aligning into regional health care networks. Regional networks are almost always smaller than competing GPOs, but their size is actually the foundation of their strength. Because they are smaller, regional networks are often much better at getting agreement from their members to standardize on a method or product for exclusive systemwide use. Standardization enhances efficiency, and the compliance to specific product use allows the network to leverage pricing with the manufacturer. Regional health care networks will continue to develop and grow, meaning that sales professionals must become adept at managing a customer system.

VALUE ANALYSIS TEAMS

The last trend impacting purchasing practices is that health care now is more oriented toward promoting wellness than treating illness. The longer a person remains sick today, the more money an HMO must spend. By keeping members well, HMOs have a greater opportunity to positively impact their bottom line. This trend has led to the development of value analysis team (VATs), which jointly review products and practices for the purpose of selecting those that can reduce patient recovery times or promote overall wellness. VATs are here to stay.

Value analysis teams make decisions as a committee comprised of clinicians and financial experts from many different parts of a health care organization. This introduces complexity into the decision-making process that salespeople are trying to understand. No longer is a rep calling on one doctor or one nurse when trying to sell a product. The rep must now manage the politics surrounding "decision by committee." VATs are basically looking at three areas or categories of questions in their review of products. Sales reps need to have the answer to these questions when presenting products to the VAT.

1. All else being equal, is the new product less expensive for our facility to use?
2. If there is no price savings, can we make the jobs of our workers easier with this new product thereby improving our labor efficiency?
3. Will this product, at no additional cost, make the work environment safer for either staff or patients?

These questions regarding cost, ease of use, and safety form the basis for product decisions made by value analysis teams.

When interviewing for a sales position, you should ask these same questions about the company's products relative to the competition in the marketplace. If the company's products are all more expensive, then they better have a functional or safety advantage. If not, you need to question whether the market will seek out and purchase the products you would be selling. "Me-too" products that mirror every aspect of the product that has been copied are very difficult to sell even if you are known for your sales savvy.

Customers in the health care marketplace will not make a change unless there is a strong reason to do so because change is very expensive. Hospital purchasing personnel have long suggested that changing from one supplier to another costs about 5 percent of the annual expense for the product line being changed. Value analysis teams need strong reasons to make a product switch, and reps must recognize the cost of change. Salespeople must be ready to demonstrate how their product's design, technology, and/or quality can improve staff efficiency, enhance the quality of care delivered, or lower supply costs.

As health care delivery continues to evolve, purchasing practices will also continue to change. Change truly is the only thing constant in health care.

CHAPTER 6

A DAY IN THE LIFE
OF A MEDICAL SALES REP

Work is life, you know, and without it, there's nothing but fear and insecurity.

John Lennon

When medical supply companies begin interviewing for a new sales position, one of the steps involved is having the job candidate ride with an experienced rep in order to give the candidate an idea of what the life of a medical rep is all about. It might be helpful, however, to have an idea what that life is like before the interview process begins. Featured below is the written diary of a medical sales rep from a Fortune 100 company. The diary includes all of the activities participated in during a one-week period. (All names have been changed, and none of the names used are intended to refer to a specific person or place in health care.)

DIARY OF A SALES REPRESENTATIVE

Monday:

5:30 A.M. Left home to drive 1 hour to first call at St. Mary's Hospital. Stopped along the way and bought donuts for surgery staff.

7:00 A.M. Held product in-service for operating room staff on new product they will begin using today. In-service lasted 30 minutes and there were 23 nurses present. They seemed excited about the product and agreed to use it for one month.

8:00 A.M. Met with OR business manager to discuss product ordering for new product and also showed new XXX.

8:30 A.M. Completed business review for a materials manager, which highlight previous quarter usage trends. Also discussed interest in XXX, which is currently supplied by competitor. He agreed to entertain a price proposal from me.

9:30 A.M. Met with unit manager of the neonatal unit to demonstrate XXX. They are using a competitive product but are not happy with it because of quality concerns. She asked me to get pricing for her and some additional samples for her doctors to review.

10:00 A.M. After completing calls at St. Mary's, drove over to Smith Surgical, our local distributor. Spent 30 minutes on the phone making appointments for Friday then met with operations manager just to make sure enough inventory had come in for the St. Mary's start-up of XXX.

11:00 A.M. Met with the facility manager at Jonesville Health Clinic. The was an initial meeting with her, and she indicated that cost containment issues are driving all product decisions in her facility. She said that she would be willing to look at any products that have the potential to reduce supply costs. Also indicated that she did not want me demonstrating any product to any end user without her prior approval. Asked her for product usage figures on competing products in order to complete an initial proposal.

12:15 P.M. Had lunch with Kevin Wilbur, the rep for Smith Surgical, to discuss target accounts on new product launch. He agreed to ask his top five accounts to evaluate XXX. He will fax me competitive product usage and pricing if he can get it.

1:30 P.M. Held short in-service for Dr. Wilson's nursing staff to review the use of XXX. Dr. Wilson has agreed to trial the product in his office, and if he likes it will also ask the hospital to buy it.

2:15 P.M.   Spent additional 30 minutes on phone making appointments. Made 6 calls and contacted 1 person.

3:00 P.M.   Initial call on lab director at Caylor Hospital to demonstrate the new XXX. They were happy with existing product and said that they were not interested in changing. Last call of the day—over at 3:25.

5:00 P.M.   After 80 miles of driving to get back home, made phone calls to two other distributor reps to ensure that they were bringing additional new items into stock for St. Patrick Hospital and University Hospital.

7:00 P.M.   Spent 45 minutes loading car for overnight trip to Wilson City. Packed enough of XXX to demonstrate on 4 calls over 2-day period. Ended day at 7:45.

Tuesday:

5:30 A.M.   Departed for 2.5-hour drive to Wilson City. Arrived in town in time for 8:00 A.M. appointment.

8:00 A.M.   Appointment with CFO at Dustin Medical Center to propose prime vendor agreement with the Medical Center. The Med Ctr. has been challenged to reduce operating expenses by 15 percent next year. They anticipate staff layoffs and are interested in any opportunities to save money. He liked the proposal and asked me to follow up with him next week. Great meeting, which ended at 9:30.

10:15 A.M. Ran late for 10:00 A.M. meeting with the labor and delivery manager at the Med Ctr. She was late as well so it worked out okay. A major competitor has been in with their XXX. She seemed to like it and was really interested in it because it was 15 percent less in price than ours. Call the office about better pricing later.

11:30 A.M. Went to a lunch meeting with the local APIC (Association for Practitioners in Infection Control) chapter. Listened to a speaker from XXX Company. Was able to meet two new infection control nurses from the area.

1:00 P.M. Met with oncology unit manager to present XXX. He did not like it at all, but said he was always willing to look at new products. Make a note to see him again in three months.

1:45 P.M. Spent an hour on phone returning customer calls and making appointments.

2:45 P.M. Final appoint at the Med Ctr. was with the sterile processing manager. She also has been looking at a competitive product. She highlighted the pressure that everyone is under to lower supply costs. I told her that I was working on a new prime vendor proposal for the hospital that would lower my product's cost in her department. She promised that she would not make any changes until she received our formal proposal.

3:15 P.M. Left the Med Ctr. and drove across town for meeting at Dr. Johnson's Orthopedic Clinic. He had seen one of our new ortho products at the national convention of orthopedic surgeons and wanted to take a look at it. After demonstrating it to him, he asked me to get some sterile samples for him to try in the hospital, and also asked me to call on the ortho head nurse at the Med Ctr.

4:30 P.M. Ran by another distributor here in Wilson City to drop off new catalogs for their customer service reps.

5:30 P.M. Checked in at hotel and followed up on phone calls to manager and Steve Miller, a local OEM rep.

6:30 P.M. Went out to dinner with Jane Lister who is the general surgery coordinator at the Med Ctr. She is a strong supporter of our products and I may need her to help champion the new prime vendor proposal we are submitting.

9:00 P.M. Back to hotel and finish up some expense reports from last week.

Wednesday:

7:00 A.M. Checked out of hotel and drove over for meeting with the environmental services manager at Bart Memorial Hospital. She is concerned with the disposal costs associated with one of our products the hospital just began using. She claims that it will cost the hospital another $2,000 annually to dispose of XXX properly, and she wants the hospital to reconsider their decision.

7:30 A.M.   Met with Judy Johnson, the infection control nurse who was primarily responsible for getting XXX into the hospital. We discussed the concerns expressed by environmental services and she indicated that it was nothing that would reverse their decision to use our product.

8:15 A.M.   Hooked up with Lisa Jackson in purchasing at Bart Memorial to see if they have had anymore back orders on XXX. We have been slow in production on this product and have had to help her find substitutes on two occasions. As of today, all orders have been filled.

9:00 A.M.   Went to local Kinko's and made copies of product literature, sent two faxes, and also made telephone calls for about 45 minutes.

11:00 A.M. Met with OR director, Nancy Ryan, at Belmont Surgery Center to present XXX. She is very interested because she feels we have a superior product. She will need help convincing the doctors who own the center to switch because our product is more expensive. She asked me to try and catch Dr. Hoffman in his office today to discuss the product differences. Had Nancy call his office to let them know that I was coming.

11:50 A.M. Was able to catch Dr. Hoffman and show him the product. The cost difference is only about $1,500 so he indicated that he would support the change!

12:30 P.M.   Began drive back home and made appointments on car phone while driving to the next account. Also, ate burgers through the drive-through.

1:30 P.M.   Stopped at Rush County Hospital to meet initially with the materials manager. Do not have any business here and the hospital is owned by Columbia. Since we do not have a contract with Columbia, John Wilson suggested we probably would not have any opportunity to do any business there. I do not plan on going back unless National Accounts does something with Columbia.

3:00 P.M.   Made final call of the day on the Diagnostic Laboratory. Received a lead here from one of our distributors. Lab manager, Jill Coleman, agreed to place a trial order provided our pricing is close to their current product.

5:00 P.M.   Got back home and spent two hours on the computer working on presentations for tomorrow, bringing weekly report up to date, and also updating customer database. Finished day at 7:00 P.M.

Thursday:

8:00 A.M.   Conducted sales meeting for sales reps and customer service reps at Smith Surgical. Went over all new product releases since last sales meeting and provided product samples they could use with customers. Introduced sales promotion program designed to reward reps who help close new business. Two-hour meeting that was very effective.

11:00 A.M. Did short product presentation to orthopedic group. Went well but didn't get much time to really cover what I needed to go over. Two of the doctors mentioned that they liked it, and the group said they would review it at a later date. I must get some support from Drs. Nephews and Flowers in order to have a shot at this business.

12:00 P.M. Lunch appointment with Gil Sanders, a local OEM rep with Regional Custom. We discussed the business at Caylor Hospital and also targeted the Thompson Medical Pavilion at the university. We will make a joint call there next week, and Gil agreed to make the necessary appointments.

1:00 P.M. Began a series of appointments at Belleview Community Hospital. The first meeting was with Jan Wilson, OR manager, and we discussed ways in which we might help them improve the utilization of our products by completing a review with her head nurses in the department. We scheduled a time for me to come in next Thursday during the afternoon to meet with them.

1:30 P.M. Met with materials management to present XXX. Don Hatch views these products as commodity products, but he did agree to switch over if we were priced lower than the current supplier. He gave me competitive code numbers and usage figures and asked me to offer a proposal when I'm back in next week.

2:15 P.M.   Appointment with Amy Mincer, manager of the emergency room. She had requested to see XXX through a professional journal. We reviewed the product and she called Don Hatch to let him know that she wanted to place an order for 2 cases. Went back down to see Don and called the distributor to make sure that they had the product in stock. Don did place the order.

3:30 P.M.   In-service for oncology unit. Reviewed new product to be used by physicians and nurses. Highlighted functional differences between current product and ours with emphasis on ease of use with our product. Staff liked the new measurement system because it eliminates faulty readings.

4:15 P.M.   Finished up day at the hospital with a quick call on Don Hatch's assistant, Mary Phillips. Mary does all of the ordering of our products for the hospital and has been complaining that she has had trouble getting some of our products through their distributor. She says that she has had no problems this week but that she will call me if anything else comes up.

6:00 P.M.   Back in my office at home to make phone calls to distributor and OEM reps. Also, loaded car and prepared all sales collateral for tomorrow. Finished the day at 7:30.

Friday:

7:00 A.M. Picked up sales manager at airport and had brief sales update for the territory and reviewed sales forecast for the next quarter.

8:00 A.M. Had first appointment with Parkside General materials manager, Will Anderson. This account has been a long-time customer and I have a standing appointment with Will every Friday at 8:00. He usually has a couple of people for me to see.

8:30 A.M. Will asked me to follow up with Beth Miller in purchasing to finalize the implementation for XXX. The need approximately 2 weeks worth of product for an initial stocking order and also need the distributor to bring committed volume into the distributor warehouse.

9:00 A.M. Meeting with Austin French, the OR director, to discuss interest in switching their XXX product line. Austin is very analytical and wanted to see performance data on all of our product as well as a complete line-item pricing analysis. We did cover all of the product data today, and he wants the pricing comparison before he takes it any further. However, he was very positive about taking a closer look.

10:00 A.M. Got a break to make phone calls and send a couple of fax follow-ups. Spent most of the time on hold but did get two appointments set for Monday.

10:45 A.M. Had brief meeting with Jennifer Coldiron, lab director. She is very unhappy with a recent change we have made in XXX. She wants to send the product back and look for something else. The change is permanent and we do not have the old product available. I arranged to come back in next week to talk to her staff about their concerns. There is a strong possibility of losing this business, but we will try to solve this next week.

12:00 P.M. Went to chapter meeting of local Association of Operating Room Nurses (AORN) for lunch. A program was presented on "Laparoscopic Instrumentation." I did hook up with one new OR director at this meeting and also saw 7 current customers. This is a monthly meeting that I regularly attend.

1:30 P.M. Met with the corporate VP for materials management for the Health Alliance of Northern Illinois, Dick Greene. This alliance consists of 8 rural hospitals totaling 1,104 beds. We have no business with this group but want to pursue it because of the committed volume they offer suppliers. All of the negotiation is done at Mr. Greene's level, but product preference is determined at the individual hospital level. They have a monthly product review meeting that is attended by the purchasing managers of each hospital.

3:00 P.M. Dropped manager off at the airport and then made it back to my office and spent the remainder of the day filling out weekly report, writing follow-up letters, and making phone calls. Finished up the week at 6:00 P.M. Friday.

SUMMARY

Each moment in the life of a medical sales rep is filled with small steps designed to constantly move the business forward. Minutes not spent in direct customer contact are usually dedicated to planning and prioritizing the next move. For those who enjoy the psychology of persuasion and the challenge of pursuit, this field will never disappoint.

CHAPTER 7

STRATEGIES FOR
CAREER PLACEMENT

In order that people may be happy in their work,
these three things are needed: They must be fit for it:
they must not do too much of it: and they must have a
sense of success in it.

W. H. Auden

After making the decision that medical sales is the
career of choice, the next step is to develop a strategy to
secure that first position. Relative to the total job population, there are not many medical sales positions available
and they are not always easy to track down. Knowing
where to find out about medical companies and various job
openings is crucial to future employment in this field. The
following resources can help identify job opportunities as
you begin the networking process needed to get your foot
in the door.

LANDING A JOB

Where Do I Start?

- Hospital Purchasing Departments
- Salespeople and Managers
- Corporate Recruiters
- Newspapers
- Medical School Libraries
- On-Line Services
- Headhunters

HOSPITAL PURCHASING DEPARTMENTS

The best place to start finding out about potential sales openings is with the customer. Every hospital, for example, has either a purchasing or materials management department that interfaces daily with hundreds of companies. The department will have a manager and possibly several purchasing agents who specialize in buying specific categories of products. These individuals are usually some of the first to know about sales openings. Additionally, they can provide the names of district sales managers and general information about companies you may have an interest in. Purchasing departments also will have product catalogs from all of the companies selling products to the hospital.

These catalogs can provide great insight into the company's products, vision, and image. Make a trip to the hospital and browse through some of these catalogs.

Since purchasing personnel work with medical companies every day, they can often provide you with the most accurate appraisal of a company's strengths and weaknesses. If you really like this field, call a purchasing manager (or a physician's office manager) and ask for information on vacant sales territories and for suggestions on which companies they would go to work for if they wanted to go into sales. Even if you do not find an immediate opening, you will get great insight into which companies might be the best for you. Also, if you do get a job in the area, you have already made a good impression on a potential customer by demonstrating thoroughness in your own decision making.

SALESPEOPLE AND MANAGERS

After you have made the purchasing contact and decided on a few companies, go ahead and call the sales manager for the local territory. Explain who you are, why you are calling, and question if their company has any vacant territories. Medical sales reps do have a "sales fraternity" and usually know of openings in other companies even if there are no immediate openings in their own. By beginning a network process with both current reps and their customers, you will quickly find available positions.

View current sales reps and managers as your customer. They ARE! A manager who has five to ten reps may not have an immediate opening where you are located but they may soon, and they also may have positions open in nearby territories that would be available to you if you are willing to relocate. Keep in mind that companies often pay recruiting firms several thousand dollars for a candidate, and if you have taken the initiative to find the opening, you could save the company that fee. If they do not have an opening, make sure to at least forward a resume and ask what qualifications they require when they are in the recruiting mode. Also, being recommended to an employer by someone already in the business goes a long way.

CORPORATE RECRUITERS

Some very large companies have their own corporate recruiters, whose sole function is to recruit talented salespeople. If you have a strong desire to work for a company with name recognition, find out if they have recruiters. You can do this by calling one of the company's reps or by calling the company directly.

Corporate recruiters do not ordinarily do any direct hiring. They will complete one or two rounds of interviews for the purpose of sending only the most qualified candidates to the sales manager who is actually filling a position. A corporate recruiter is much different from an independent recruiter or headhunter. The corporate recruiter is searching for the best candidate, and a headhunter is trying to sell a company on the idea that they have already found the best person for the job. Headhunters will be covered later, but for now just remember that in this industry the average annual turnover is approximately 20 percent, and paying a recruiting fee to fill each open position is not something companies want to do.

Keep in mind also that even though a company may not have a full-time recruiter, it may still offer some incentive to its sales employees to recruit new reps. It is much less expensive for a company to give some stock or small cash payment to its own employees than to hire an outside employment agency. Companies that do reward their reps with recruitment incentives have virtually as many corporate recruiters as they do employees. Find out who they are and get to know them.

A few companies have newsletters that highlight key product introductions and list territory openings; other market segments have professional sales journals. One such journal is the *Pharmaceutical Representative* published by McKnight Medical Communications. These journals can not be purchased in a retail setting or found in a library, so be sure to ask reps that you have contacted to send past issues to you or call and subscribe. The more contacts you make, the better your chances of finding a position.

NEWSPAPERS

Nearly every metropolitan newspaper will advertise some type of medical sales job every weekend. Most positions advertised in the paper are pharmaceutical sales openings, and because most of these positions are entry-level positions, there will be a lot of competition involved. Unbelievably, a pharmaceutical position advertised in a major U.S. city can draw as many as 2,000 resumes! From those 2,000 a company might interview only forty-five to fifty candidates. Recognizing that your chances of just getting an interview are less than 3 percent, your qualifications must be exactly what the company is looking for, and they must be presented in a unique way that would generate interest.

Newspapers offer an easy way of identifying job openings, but many people competing with you for the job have easily discovered the same position. Also, because the advertisement may only give a P.O. box for the return address, finding out who the company is and the name of the person doing the hiring might be impossible through the newspaper alone. That is when the three methods of identifying job opportunities just described can help improve your chances of being one of the fifty asked to come in for the interview. Companies are always impressed with individuals who have worked very hard to find out about the company and the position. Newspapers are a great source of information, but they are only a starting point.

MEDICAL SCHOOL LIBRARIES

Every medical school in the country has an on-site medical library. Although most of the periodicals and journals are written specifically for physicians, medical students, and nurses, some of them are also written for paramedical professionals such as materials managers, purchasing agents, and supply technicians. Publications such as *Hospital Purchasing News* or *Modern Healthcare* will include information on companies and products, new GPO contracts, and management changes in medical product companies.

Even journals written specifically for the health care practitioner often include company advertisements and specific product information. You probably won't find sales openings listed, but you will improve your understanding of the market and develop a better idea of which companies you really want to pursue. There are also specific journals that discuss the business aspect of health care. Reading these can help you develop a better overall understanding of the market and give you an edge over those you are competing with for a sales position.

If you can not find a medical school library, most hospitals have their own libraries that you may be able to access. These are much smaller versions of the medical school library, but they do contain most of the popular health care management journals. If all else fails, the local public library will be able to provide basic financial information on medical supply companies.

ON-LINE SERVICES

Services such as CompuServe and America Online provide a wealth of career placement information that can help with your resume writing and job search. George Washington University, for instance, has a site known as "The Job Search Process," which covers everything from business letter writing to professional networking. Additionally, financial information on companies you are interested in can be retrieved from areas such as Hoover's or Morningstar. Annual reports, historical stock performance, and broker analyses also can be obtained.

The Internet, too, can provide job placement services. By requesting a search of "Medical Sales" or "Sales Recruiting" from your web browser, you will be able to identify websites that will include sales placement firms specializing in the medical field as well as medical companies that actually post sales positions on-line. Companies such as Medtronic (www.medtronic.com) for example, will list available sales positions on their home page in an effort to reduce their sales recruiting expenses.

The Internet will become more important to medical companies in the future as they realize that it is an easy way for customers to access critical information they need in their decision-making process. The government is already a big user of the Internet and provides career guidance through such services as the Occupational Profiles Database. This database even provides a list of State Employment Security Agencies and State Occupational Information Coordinating Committees, which can provide you with information on state and local job markets and additional career information.

HEADHUNTERS

Headhunters are independent recruiters who serve employers in an effort to find the most qualified candidate for an open sales position. They are contracted to perform a search and do not work directly for the company doing the hiring. In this field, medical recruiters are always paid by the employer. If you want to get into this field and a recruiter indicates that you must pay in order for the search to begin, find another recruiter. Do not pay someone to begin a job search for you. Medical companies may pay $5,000 or more to a headhunter for a recruit, and it is not necessary for you to pay any extra.

There are a couple of things to keep in mind if you are considering working with a recruiter. First, recognize that unless they have a long-term relationship with specific companies, headhunters find out about job openings in the same way that you do (i.e., the six methods of finding job opportunities just described). Granted, they probably have established contacts for doing their research, but if you can find out about the same opportunities on your own, you have an advantage over a candidate that they might send to an interviewing company. If your qualifications are similar to the candidate that they send, you win because there is no recruiting price tag associated with your hiring. That should be a great incentive to network with others already in the field.

On the positive side, if the recruiter has an established record of success in recruiting for a specific company, the company may never advertise the opening in any other way than through the recruiter. In these instances, headhunters become the sole gatekeepers of who gets interviewed. Recruiters do perform a valuable service, and the expense is often worth it because they can reduce the amount of downtime in a territory without any representation by constantly having a supply of candidates available. The recruiter also can eliminate the high cost associated with a sales manager's travel to an area in search of a candidate. It is often much easier for a manager to interview five candidates who have been screened by a recruiter than it is to sift through hundreds of resumes and applications that have been received as a result of a newspaper ad.

Medical sales recruiters are not always easy to find because they do not typically advertise in traditional mediums. As a matter of fact, many of them do not advertise at all because their job is to locate and recruit talent, not wait for it to come to them. However, you can find recruiters by asking other reps if they were placed in their jobs by one. Also, some of them do advertise their services on the Internet and in professional journals.

Most recruiters in this field are sole proprietors or partner-managed businesses, and they normally recruit for the entire country. Even though you may live on the East Coast, it is very possible that a recruiter on the West Coast could provide you with the best opportunities in your area. Your only contact with the recruiter may be over the telephone, so always be prepared to show your energy, organization, and communication skills when he or she calls.

If you approach a professional recruiter, be prepared to go through an interview process similar to what you would go through with an employer. The recruiter's reputation is based on the quality of the candidate he or she sends to an interview, and that recruiter will want to make sure that you have the necessary qualifications and interview skills. Expect also to provide written documentation of your achievements as well as complete personality profile testing by the recruiter. In essence, treat the recruiter just like you would a potential employer since you are asking him or her to become your number one salesperson. A recruiter's livelihood is based on his or her ability to sell talent to an employer.

SUMMARY

Landing a position in medical sales requires probing, patience, and persistence, the same attributes necessary for success once you begin the job. No single method exists for getting into this industry, but those who succeed utilize a combination of all the resources highlighted in this chapter. Individuals have worked as long as five years in order to get started, but using all of the resources from hospital purchasing departments to headhunters will decrease the amount of time it takes for you to find the job you want. Rest assured that if you can get the job, you can do the job.

CHAPTER 8

THE INTERVIEW AND THE DECISION

Questions are never indiscreet. Answers sometimes are.

Oscar Wilde

THE INTERVIEW PROCESS

Interviewing for a job can generate fear among even the most confident of job seekers. When the position you desire requires strong communication skills, the pressure to say the right thing at the right time is extraordinary. Interviewing for a sales position is pressure packed since it is actually the first sales presentation of your new career and your first assignment is to sell yourself. As your customer, you will find that the interviewer can be delightful or downright nasty. Some managers and recruiters do their best to put you at ease, while others want to know immediately how you will respond to a negative environment. Always be prepared for either.

The interview process usually consists of several steps. The initial step may be a phone interview, which provides both you and the employer the opportunity to screen each other for basic requirements. The second step is an initial interview where both parties have a chance to describe in detail what each is looking for and how one might fill the needs of the other. During this time, the employer may also ask the candidate to submit a formal employment application and fill out additional forms describing previous job experiences and duties. The third step is usually an interview with another individual from the company in order to give the manager a second opinion. This person may be another sales representative or it could be another manager. This step will sometimes include spending a day with an experienced rep in order to give the candidate an opportunity to see what the job is like on a day-to-day basis. It also gives the company a chance to see the candidate interact with customers.

A fourth step in the process is an additional interview with the person who would be your immediate supervisor. The purpose of this interview is to clarify any concerns that either of you may have and to probe into anything that the employer may perceive as a problem area. After this, the next step is usually a trip to the corporate office to meet various members of the sales and marketing team. When you make it this far, it usually means that the manager has made a preliminary decision to extend an offer to you but simply needs the final approval. The office visit is crucial because it not only serves as an opportunity for senior management to give their stamp of approval, but it also sets the tone for all future communication you will have with them if and when you do get the job.

The final step in the interview process is the offer itself. The offer should include base pay, the commission plan, the benefits package, and any additional incentive programs the company may have. Reserve any negotiation for this phase and ask that all promises and conditions be put in writing. Make sure that you have a clear understanding of how the company's sales commission program operates, and also ask about the qualifications for any additional incentive programs, such as bonus gift and/or trip packages that the company may offer.

Planning for the interview is critical to successful interviewing. Since an interview is a sales call, use the same type of preparation you would for calling on a potential customer. Map your travel to the interview site, study the employer's needs, develop a theme for your presentation, ask others what they know about the customer, and so on. The preparation you do for the interview is an indicator of the preparation you would go through before calling on all of your customers. Planning for the presenting you will do in the interview consists of two basic exercises:

1. documenting your previous performance
2. preparing answers to employer questions

The first step is fairly easy, and probably the best way to document your performance is to create a personal portfolio. The portfolio, often referred to as an "atta boy/girl" file, should include the following information, as well as any additional accolades that you believe document significant achievements and abilities:

- letters of commendation from previous employers
- sales performance reports from other sales jobs
- previous performance reviews
- photocopies of external degrees and training programs
- photocopies of prior awards (yes, even plaques and trophies)
- photocopies of previous W-2s
- updated resume
- college transcript

Prepare the portfolio as if you were creating marketing materials for a company product, recognizing that *you* are the product. Place all of the material inside a leather presentation binder and also take an extra copy to leave behind. The portfolio can serve as an official document of your achievements and also remind the interviewer of your skills when trying to decide who to ask back for the next interview.

The second area is preparing to answer questions you will be asked during the interview. There will always be a surprise question or two, but the more you practice answering the questions you are likely to get, the more you will come across as thoughtful and well spoken. The remainder of this chapter is dedicated to examining some of the questions you will encounter. These questions are taken from a study that asked interviewers to respond to the question, "What are the ten most frequent questions you ask job candidates?" Questions asked of salespeople generally fall into the following categories:

1. personal/career objectives
2. goal setting and achievement
3. problem solving and priority setting
4. influencing others

Be prepared to provide specific examples of work and/or extracurricular activities that demonstrate your accomplishments in each of these areas.

INTERVIEW QUESTIONS BY CATEGORY

Personal/Career Objectives

What are your long-term career objectives?
What are your short-term career objectives?
Why do you want to go into medical sales?
Are you willing to relocate?
What has led to your interest in medical sales?
Do you have any desire to move into management? Why or why not?

Why do you think that medical sales is a good career for you?

What are your impressions of our company and our industry?

How would you describe our company?

Why are you interested in our company?

How and why do you think that you would fit in with our company?

What do you think about our competition?

Why are you interested in leaving your current field and company?

What questions do you have about our company?

What are your plans for continued development and education?

What are your salary requirements?

Please relate your background to this position.

List three words that best describe you.

What portion of your job is the most rewarding to you and why?

Describe your dream job.

What work activities do you like? dislike?

Goal Setting and Achievement

How do you define success?

What motivates you to put forth your greatest effort?

Give an example of a time when you set a goal for yourself and explain how you met that goal.

How do you feel about someone else setting your goals for you?

How did you go about getting your last job?

Explain some personal goal you have had and why you wanted to accomplish that goal.

What are your strengths? weaknesses?

Tell me about your last performance evaluation.

What motivates you?

What discourages you?

How do you react when an unrealistic goal has been set for you?

What is the most difficult thing you have ever had to do? Explain how you were able to do it.

Describe a situation where you assumed responsibility for some task only because you knew it had to be done.

What is your biggest distraction from work?

Explain your priorities in life.

Give an example of a situation where you have had to prioritize several activities and explain how you went about it.

Describe the follow-up you think customers in our business would expect.

Describe a normal workday.

Describe what you do on a day off.

Are you involved in any community or civic activities? What are they and why are you committed?

Explain your choices of a college, a major field of study, and extracurricular studies.

What accomplishments in life are you most proud of and
why?

If I were to invite two people back for a second interview,
why should I choose you?

How would your previous employers describe your work
habits?

What makes you stand out from the crowd?

Problem Solving and Priority Setting

How do you organize your day?

How do you approach solving a problem?

How do you react to quick-tempered individuals?

Describe a situation where someone else faced a problem
and you helped find a solution.

Describe a situation where you have had to do lots of follow-up in order to solve some problem.

How would you rate your writing and analytical abilities?

What do you do when a customer has a problem with one of
your products?

Give an example of a customer problem that you helped
overcome.

Sometimes everyone has to break the rules. Tell me about
the time when you had to break the rules.

What would you do if someone accused you of something
that you did not do?

Tell me about a situation that caused you the most pressure
recently and how you worked it out.

What problems did you face in college?

What were the biggest challenges in your last job?

Describe any major "life" obstacles that you have had to find solutions for.

Explain your philosophy on how to handle difficult people.

What do you do when you are asked to do something you have never done before?

What will your attitude be if you do not progress in this job as you think you should?

How would you describe the ideal boss?

Tell me about the toughest decision you have had to make in the last year.

What things have you been asked to do at your current job that you find frustrating?

Give an example that indicates that you are a self-starter.

What in your background would make you successful in coping with continuing pressure and constantly changing practices?

Influencing Others

Describe how you have persuaded someone to take an action you wanted them to take.

Who is the most difficult person you ever had to persuade to your point of view?

Describe your ability to meet and deal with people of diverse backgrounds.

How would you rate your writing and analytical abilities?

What do you do when your ideas are opposed by someone who controls your success?

What leadership activities have you been involved in outside of work?

Explain how you would approach a doctor to look at a product that competes with the one he or she has been using successfully for fifteen years.

What do you think makes a good sales rep?

Explain a situation where you faced open opposition to your ideas, and yet you were able to obtain what you wanted.

Describe what methods you use to persuade others to your point of view.

Site some specific examples of leadership and communication skills.

What do you think is the most effective way to approach someone who does not want to be approached?

What is it about you that allows you to persuade others?

Describe the best salesperson you have ever met.

Why do you want to go into medical sales?

Give an example of having to persuade a group of people to your point of view.

Sell me on you.

Practice your interviewing skills by giving these questions to a friend and have him or her ask the questions in random order to help you develop strong answers with a feel of spontaneity.

The two basic requirements for effective answering of interview questions in the medical field may be no different than any other field, but they are vital to both the interview and the job. Effective answers must be based on honesty and accuracy. These two are distinct yet inseparable qualities for a successful career in medical sales.

An individual may be able to get a job by being dishonest about qualifications or previous job experience, but in the long run, dishonesty disqualifies one for a medical sales position because inaccurate information can have long-standing legal ramifications. If a representative tells a doctor that a drug can perform in a certain way or does not have some known side effect in order to close the sale, the representative (and company represented) is liable for the faulty information.

Dishonesty in the interview setting only prolongs the inevitable, and if you think it is necessary to shade reality in an interview in order to give the answer that you think the interviewer wants, you probably would not be happy in the job anyway. Answer all the questions with the intention of a truthful meeting of the minds, and do not worry about what you think the interviewer wants to hear. It is possible to overanalyze a question. For example, whenever a manager asks, "What are your career goals?", most answer with, "I want to go into management," thinking that this surely must be the answer the manager is looking for. In reality, the manager may be able to promote only one rep over a two-year period and the other seven reps still under the manager's direction must continue in their sales positions. If all eight reps want to become managers, seven of them will be very unhappy. Consequently, a manager may want to fill an open territory with an individual who wants to remain a career representative. If, however, you mention that you desire management (when you really just wanted a career position), you eliminate yourself from the manager's candidate list.

Answer all questions with honesty *and* accuracy. Interviewers are very skilled at finding empty periods of employment or spotting negative performance from previous jobs and they will ask about those situations. Accuracy in the job is essential and they want to see it during the interview as well. Your accurate assessment of why you had six months of unemployment will be more impressive than an answer filled with inaccurate excuses and finger pointing toward a previous employer. Accuracy in every answer demonstrates that you will precisely report expenses, forecast sales, and manage account information.

DECIDING ON A JOB

A final recommendation in the interviewing and job selection process is that you always plan two jobs ahead of the one you are trying to secure. The result of this approach is twofold. First, it makes you plan your career beyond a single position, and interviewers will give special consideration for that kind of forward thinking. Second, this approach requires that you must ask, "Will this job help me to get to the position I want later?" If taking the job you are interviewing for will get you no closer to the position you want to be in two jobs from now, you should not take the position. It is quite possible that the job you are pursuing is your dream job, and if that is the case you are not concerned about a job two positions later. Your concern is simply, "Will I be happy in this position permanently?" In this instance, take the time to quantify the job traits necessary to qualify the position as your dream job. A general consideration is that a dream job is one in which you would enjoy spending the rest of your life. Very few people view entry-level sales positions as their final career destination, so it is also important to know what career options are available in the medical field after the joy wanes in that first job. Chapter 9 is dedicated to career advancement options for the medical sales professional, and it is designed to help you see yourself two jobs from now.

CHAPTER 9

CAREER ADVANCEMENT

The most successful career must show a waste of
strength that might have removed mountains, and the
most unsuccessful is not that of the man who is taken
unprepared, but of him who has prepared is never
taken. On a tragedy of that kind our national morality
is duly silent.

E. M. Forster

The road to job satisfaction begins with locating and se-
curing the most desirable job. Long-term professional con-
tentment, however, hinges upon developing a vision that
includes a well-designed career plan. There are many career
development options available to anyone who begins a
career in medical sales. Some of these opportunities are in
other sales positions, but many of them exist outside of the
classic sales path. Advancement into positions beyond
entry-level sales should be reviewed and planned for long
before the actual placement opportunity arrives.

Entry-level sales positions can lead to virtually any corporate position that exists provided the salesperson has the right background and training. Sales employees generally do not gravitate toward the more exact technical positions such as manufacturing or research and development. Instead, they tend to remain on one of three primary advancement tracks. They are:

- sales track
- sales management track
- marketing track

Each track can be differentiated by the respective approach to the customer. The sales track keeps individuals in direct contact with the customer and in charge of all sales activities at the account level. Those on the sales management track interact with the customer indirectly by managing the sales activities of representatives. Finally, the marketing track requires that customer contact be initiated and maintained indirectly through the process of product development.

Outlined below are the basic career advancement tracks available to the entry-level medical sales representative. It is possible to change from one track to another, and many companies do encourage cross-tracking in order to develop employees that have a broad understanding of their businesses. Consider the tracks and positions that exist in each:

Sales Track	Sales Management Track	Marketing Track
Senior Sales Positions	Training	Product Management
National Accounts	Management	Market Research
Corporate Accounts	OEM Management	New Business Development
International Sales	Distributor Management	Corporate Relations

For those who believe that selling is life, that competition is the key to progress, the sales track is the only one to consider. Every position in this track is responsible for sales results in some form or fashion. If you love the challenge of selling, make sure you know what advanced sales opportunities will exist for you later in your career with a company.

SALES TRACK

Senior Sales Positions

The larger medical supply companies (more than $100 million in annual sales) will have opportunities for their salespeople to advance without requiring them to move out of their existing territories. If you consider yourself a career sales representative, investigate what additional sales responsibilities can be assumed with the company. Reps with a history of strong sales performance are often given promotions to positions such as senior sales representative or senior account manager. The promotion will include an increase in base pay plus additional responsibilities, such as assisting with new product test markets or in field sales training.

A few companies will even have a third sales level such as executive account representative (or some similar title), which allows for additional pay and job responsibility. The position may require that the rep become a mentor for new reps and serve in the capacity of an assistant sales manager. Companies with such career options for those who want to remain salespeople always have higher retention rates than companies that do not.

National Accounts

The national account position is one that requires the rep to call on hospital group purchasing organizations, for-profit hospital chains, and/or retail and wholesale chains. More and more medical supply business is controlled through contacts negotiated by national account teams, and consequently the sales pressure in this position is immense. Individual contracts with GPOs, for example, range into the millions of dollars.

Companies have national account sales teams consisting of personnel who have been promoted to the position based on outstanding sales results in an individual territory. The number of total national account positions will range from 5 to 10 percent of the total number of sales positions. In the current market, product lines that are sold directly to or prescribed by physicians are least likely to be sold through national account contracts. Products that are purchased through hospitals or other health care facilities are highly likely to be affected by national agreements. If you have a desire to work in a high-impact sales area, look for those companies with existing national account positions, or at least products that lend themselves to national agreements.

National account managers are responsible for both contract negotiation and implementation. They must establish a long-term sales action plan for their accounts since many national agreements are negotiated only once every four to five years. They are also responsible for presenting product features and benefits, establishing the terms and conditions of contracts, developing a sales force action plan per contract, conducting timely business reviews, and managing GPO sales personnel. Positions in national accounts are the most well-paid sales positions available because of the amount of business they generate with new contacts. Simply put, selling to national accounts is a high risk, high reward activity!

Corporate Accounts

The only significant difference between a national account and a corporate account position is the size of the customer. Corporate account sales positions are responsible for signing contracts with entities such as regional health care alliances and networks. These networks, which may also include health maintenance organizations, represent much smaller business opportunities for medical companies, but they do demand special attention from dedicated salespeople.

International Sales

The opportunity to move from an entry-level sales position to an international sales position is growing rapidly because U.S. companies continue to expand their presence in international markets. Obviously, multilingual reps have an edge over reps who speak only English, and many companies offer company-sponsored education that could be used to learn another language. International positions are highly sought after because the pay is excellent and in some cases nontaxable.

SALES MANAGEMENT TRACK

Ronald Reagan once said, "Surround yourself with the best people you can find, delegate authority, and don't interfere." Sales management is primarily an exercise in finding good people and motivating them to do their jobs. Sales managers are like coaches in that they are ultimately responsible to the company for the performance of their sales teams.

Medical sales companies average one sales manager for every eight to ten representatives, or 10 to 12 percent of the total sales force, and there may be another management layer that each frontline manager must report to under a national sales manager or vice president of sales. There are also some additional management positions available in this track. A sales organizational chart would look something like this:

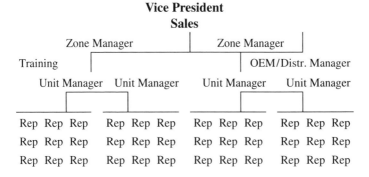

Each sales management position has distinct responsibilities.

Training

Field training and classroom training are the locations where training takes place in a sales organization. Field trainers do exactly what the name implies. They travel to a specific representative's territory and offer specialized training without the rep having to miss valuable sales time in the field. These trainers may report directly to the VP of sales or, in some cases, each manager under the VP may have a dedicated field sales trainer for all of the reps in the area. Trainers do not have direct sales responsibility (commission earnings may be limited because of this), and companies usually use the trainer position in order to groom a person for their first management job.

Classroom training in a company's corporate office is coordinated by a training manager and completed by full-time trainers and guest trainers from the sales and sales management team. Training for new reps is always necessary due to the annual turnover that occurs as a result of promotion, termination, or voluntary exit. Classroom training is much like schoolwork, so if you enjoy teaching, training may be an avenue you should pursue.

Training can be categorized into either sales training or product training and both are vital to medical sales. Sales training emphasizes listening skills, handling objections, communication skills, persuasive selling, and so on without regard to specific products or services. This type of training seeks simply to improve one's ability to initiate buying activities, and it is helpful throughout a salesperson's career even if they leave the company where the training was given.

Product training is designed to educate salespeople on all of the functional and technical properties of the company's products. This training provides analyses of competitive products and, most importantly, an understanding of the market in which specific products are sold. While sales strategy training is more philosophical in its approach, product training is much more technical because it requires precise handling of product application and medical indications. There are not many training positions available relative to the entire sales population, but because the length of time people spend in such positions is short (two years or fewer), the opportunity to move into training is good.

Management

Sales manager positions in medical sales are challenging due to the fact that your subordinates and superiors ultimately become your customers and both must be satisfied. This demanding position is responsible for these key areas:

- sales coaching
- recruiting
- performance appraisal
- administration

High performance in each area is critical to the long-term success of the company.

SALES COACHING

Sales coaching represents the biggest demand on a manager's time. Because it involves working with reps in their own territories, manager positions are high-travel jobs requiring as many as four to five overnights per week. The coaching function is designed to provide sales direction and sales correction. In order to determine whether a sales strategy is working, every rep has to be presenting the same vision of the company. The manager must make sure that reps are presenting a consistent perspective.

RECRUITING

The recruiting function can monopolize a manager whenever an opening exists, so the best approach to recruiting is to make sure that sales coaching is so effective that no one wants to leave and the company is pleased with every rep's performance. Recruiting involves working with headhunters, corporate recruiters, employee referrals, and hundreds of letters and resumes. Interviewing, background checks, and implementation of human resource policies are just a few of the recruiting activities that a sales manager must complete. A bad hiring decision can cost a company hundreds of thousands of dollars when you consider the investment a company makes in a rep's salary and training plus the loss of new sales during the training period. Recruiting the right people affects the ability to achieve sales results and control expenses more than any other management activity.

PERFORMANCE APPRAISAL

The prospect of a performance appraisal usually strikes fear in the hearts of those undergoing the review, but it creates just as much conflict for the manager responsible for completing the review. In the best case, managers will work with one rep thirty-five to forty days annually. They must accurately assess the rep's performance even though they spend less than 10 percent of their work hours with that rep. Each work session with the rep becomes very important and the manager must be able to develop an effective review based on the observations made during each coaching session. The paperwork involved with a review is tedious because each criteria reviewed must include examples of specific activities being performed as well as a complete accounting of a rep's sales versus objective.

ADMINISTRATION

Administrative duties include reviewing all paperwork completed at the rep level, assisting reps with career development plans, reporting coaching results to superiors and reps, and reporting team sales activities and results. The paperwork of a manager is usually a function of the paperwork required of one rep times the number of reps a manager is responsible for. Unfortunately, since most normal working hours are spent coaching, managers spend many weeknight and weekend hours doing paperwork and completing other administrative duties.

Managing requires the effective deployment of all available company resources. Expenses are incurred daily for entertainment, travel, company cars, sales training, computers, and so forth, and managers are responsible for how company dollars are spent on those items. The most expensive resource a company has, however, is its people, and sales managers have the responsibility to produce sales results with this invaluable resource.

OEM/Distributor Management

Medical supply companies sell such a large percentage of their products through original equipment manufacturers and distributors that full-time positions exist to manage these businesses. These are sales management positions since a primary job activity is to assist OEM and distributor companies in managing their sales efforts. Additional responsibilities include developing sales incentive programs, managing sales samples and literature, coordinating sales efforts between two sales forces, establishing price concessions, and eliminating competition. OEM managers, for example, must wear the hats of sales and management. They must reach preestablished sales targets to the OEM and then help the OEM manage the sale of the company's products to the end user.

MARKETING TRACK

Marshall McLuhan, the well known Canadian communications theorist, said that "Advertising is the greatest art form of the twentieth century." Advertising is only a part of marketing, but McLuhan alludes to the idea that marketing is certainly not an exact science, it is art! Advertising is really nothing more than the process of making a promise believable, while marketing is involved with deciding what promise needs to be made and how to go about fulfilling it.

Several areas exist in the medical field for those interested in the marketing track.

Product Management

Most marketers in the medical field are known as product managers because they are completely responsible for a single product or product line from the point of inception to the point of sale. Product managers are responsible for bringing a product to life. This involves listening to customer needs to determine product development opportunities. Additionally, the manager must assist in designing a product that will do what the customer wants at a price that is beneficial to both the company's profit objectives and the customer's financial constraints.

Product managers interface with research and development, accounting and finance, purchasing, shipping and distribution, outside vendors, and manufacturing in order to design, manufacture, and sell the product. They must manage products in much the same way sales managers handle people. The average product in the United States has an approximate life span of seven years. Medical products change even faster because medical procedures and technologies change so rapidly. The introduction of a new product is the result of efforts from many different departments and the use of various company resources. A marketing product manager is in charge of a product's design, development, and deployment with the express purpose of meeting a market need while returning a profit to the company.

Market Research

Market research is different from marketing research. Marketing research is usually a responsibility of a product manager, and it is the process of determining how to best present a product to the marketplace in order to maximize sales. Market research, however, is more customer focused because all of the research that is done is for the purpose of understanding the conditions of the market exactly as they are now and how they will be in the future. Market researchers work closely with customer focus groups, which are panels consisting of nurses, physicians, and health care technicians. If you are a great listener, creative, and really enjoy problem solving, market research positions are for you.

New Business Development

Marketers specializing in new business development are the sleuths of marketing because their primary efforts are aimed at finding new markets for existing products, creating subtle changes in existing products so they can be used in a different application, or uncovering new products that can be made with existing manufacturing technologies. Listening skills again are very important in these positions. The decision to alter an existing product to meet the needs of a different market (i.e., changing the case count of a hospital product so that it can be sold in the home health market) can result in stagnant inventory if the research is incomplete or inaccurate.

Some of the most successful products ever invented ended up being used for an application other than the one for which they were originally intended. Market researchers look for those unusual applications and spend most of their time trying to understand the market so that they can communicate needs to product developers and design engineers.

Corporate Relations

A person in corporate relations is responsible for seeing the forest instead of the trees and must communicate that vision to potential customers and stockholders. Large corporations have community relations experts, media specialists, and company spokespersons who are all responsible for marketing the company, not a product. The position also is responsible for internal communications such as newsletters and financial reports.

SUMMARY OF CAREER TRACKS

The three career advancement tracks discussed are not the only careers available in a medical company. There are others such as regulatory affairs and human resources that have not even been discussed. Most people who begin with a medical company in sales, however, tend to pursue advancement in sales, sales management, or marketing. Deciding on a career path before you begin interviewing is an excellent idea because it allows you to be more precise when answering questions regarding long-term career objectives.

During the interview process, find out what really drives the business of the company. Companies make product, sales strategy, and marketing decisions based on whether the company is manufacturing driven, marketing driven, or sales driven, and the driving force behind the company can enhance or diminish your career plans depending upon what that force is.

Manufacturing-driven companies are driven by their existing expertise and manufacturing facilities. If they have large amounts of capital tied up in machines that are being underutilized, you can bet that they will spend all of their product development time trying to find a way to make other products on that machine. This approach tends to have a backward view of the market, and the challenge is to keep from being left behind by market changes.

Marketing-driven companies are pushed by what customers will need in the future. These companies are constantly trying to be innovative by keeping new products in the R&D pipeline that meet the changing needs of customers brought on by new medical techniques. A marketing focus means that a company is trying to develop products that will put them ahead of existing technologies and competition. This approach tends to have a forward view of the market, and the challenge here is to resist selling something that does not yet exist.

Sale-driven companies usually ask, "What does the customer need today?" They are run under the philosophy that, "Whatever the customer is buying is what we should be selling." Companies with this focus tend to buy other businesses or product lines whenever their customers need something that they do not have. Although it is nice to be that responsive, this approach looks only at the here and now, and the challenge is to avoid buying companies and products that will be outdated very shortly.

Each focus has advantages and disadvantages. Ideally, the best company to work for is one that integrates all three approaches into its business. As a future employee, your job is to decide whether your career plans can coexist with the focus of the company. If you want to pursue the marketing track, you will not be happy with a manufacturing-driven company because your analysis of the market will be limited to what the company can already do. If you want to stay in sales your entire career, a marketing-driven company may drive you crazy with too many changes in sales approaches and product development. If you prefer the steady environment found with a manufacturing focus, a sales-driven company will give you nightmares because everyone else always wants something different.

Deciding on a specific company or a particular field to specialize in is difficult for sales professionals because little information exists regarding many of the sales careers that are available. Salespeople are always interested in selling something that is fun to sell and that pays that highly sought after six-figure income. The field of medical sales provides the opportunity to sell high-tech, life-saving products to some of the most intelligent and demanding people on the planet. This field also affords representatives many different career advancement possibilities. The positions are there for those whose action matches their ambition. Carl Kell, a former communications professor and author, once said, "Do what you want to do in life, and someone is bound to pay you for it!"

HEALTH CARE ASSOCIATIONS

The following associations can provide information on the state of health care as well as technical information about medical practice. These resources can be used to learn health care basics important to performing as a sales representative.

American Health Care Association
1201 L Street, NW
Washington, DC 20005
202–842–4444

American Hospital Association
1840 North Lakeshore Drive
Chicago, IL 60611
800–621–6902

American Medical Association
515 North State Street
Chicago, IL 60610
312–464–5000

American Pharmaceutical Association
2215 Constitution Avenue, NW
Washington, DC 20037
202–628–4410

Association of Operating Room Nurses
  2170 South Parker Road
  Denver, CO 80231
  303–755–6300

The Certified Medical Representatives Institute
  4950 Brambleton Avenue
  Roanoke, VA 24018
  800–274–2674

Health Industry Distributors Association
  225 Reinekers Lane
  Suite 350
  Alexandria, VA 22314
  703–549–4432
  (Puts out annual directory of companies)

Health Industry Manufacturers Association
  1200 G Street, NW
  Suite 400
  Washington, DC 20005
  202–783–8700

National Association of Pharmaceutical Manufacturers
  747 Third Avenue
  New York, NY 10017
  212–838–3720

National Association of Professional Saleswomen
  1730 North Lynn Street
  Suite 502
  Arlington, VA 22209
  703–812–8642

Pharmaceutical Manufacturers Association
  1100 Fifteenth Street, NW
  Washington, DC 20005
  202–835–3400

Pharmaceutical Service Representative Association
  16195 N.W. Spyglass Drive
  Beaverton, OR 97006

SELECTED READING

AHA Guide to the Healthcare Field. Chicago: American Hospital Association, annual.

Billian's Hospital Blue Book. Atlanta: annual.

Dun's Guide to Healthcare Companies. Parsippany, NJ: Dun's Marketing Service.

Gonyea, James C. *The On-Line Job Search Companion.* New York: McGraw-Hill, Inc., 1994.

Harkay, Michael. *The 100 Best Companies to Sell For.* New York: John Wiley and Sons, 1989.

Hospital Phone Book. New Providence, RI: Reed Reference Publishing, annual.

Myerson, Richard J. *Is Selling for You?* Dover, MA: Pine Publications, 1992.

ORPD, 1996 OR Products Directory. Denver: AORN Customer Service, annual.

Peterson's Job Opportunities in Health Care. Princeton, NJ: Peterson's Guides, 1996.

Petras, Kathryn and Ross Petras. *Jobs 96.* New York: Simon and Schuster, 1995.

Pharmaceutical Marketers Directory. Boca Raton, FL: CPS Communications, annual.

Wood, Steven. *The Job Hunter's Yellow Pages.* Harleysville, PA: Career Communications, Inc., 1995.

APPENDIX C

INTERNET RESOURCES

You could spend hours reviewing information on the Internet relative to the health care industry. Most of the information is related to the practice of health care, but there is also quality information available that directly involves the medical sales field. The Internet sites listed are divided into four basic categories:

1. Health Care Recruiters on the Internet
2. Additional Employment Resources
3. Professional and Government Health Care Organizations
4. Selected Interesting Sites

In addition to the sites listed, other sites can be found using one of several available Internet search engines. You can search for selected topics with the help of:

- Alta Vista—www.altavista.digital.com/
- Hot Bot—www.hotbot.com/
- Lycos—www.lycos.com/
- MetaCrawler—www.metacrawler.cs.washington.edu: 8080/

- WebCrawler—www.webcrawler.com/
- Yahoo—www.yahoo.com/

Try typing in "medical sales," "pharmaceutical sales," or "recruiter" in the search field and visit sites that interest you. There are many additional search engines available on the Internet in addition to those previously listed. Other search engines can be found at:

www.technomax.com/etc/engines.html

This site lists 470 search engines with many tied directly to the health care field. Seventy health care search engines can be found at:

www.technomax.com/etc/1empeng.html

HEALTH CARE RECRUITERS ON THE INTERNET

There are a small number of recruiters on the Internet that specialize in medical sales. Although recruiter websites are designed to generate business for the recruiter, you will find excellent information on conducting job searches, employer/employee profiles, and sales openings.

Hero Sales Recruiting
www.webemporium.com/hero/home.html

Hero specializes in medical and pharmaceutical sales positions in the Southeast.

May Associates Executive Search
www.careerconnection.com/

This firm does include a medical sales position profile at:

www.careerconnection.com/medical.html

MedSearch Career Services Group
www.webcom.com/scope/medsearch/jobservi.html

MedSearch specializes in medical sales recruiting for the entire country. This site also provides the job seeker with additional information on the top medical companies for which to work.

SHS
www.shsinc.com/jobs.htm

This firm recruits for sales positions in several industries, but SHS does list medical sales positions on their website.

ADDITIONAL EMPLOYMENT RESOURCES

Employment Opportunities and Job Resources on the Internet
www.jobtrak.com/jobguide/

This site, run by Margaret Riley, is a guide to using the Internet in order search for a position.

Employment Resources on the Internet
www.cs.purdue.edu/homes/swlodin/jobs.html

This website contains a guide to additional employment opportunities listed on the Internet.

Internet Sales Listings
www.the-spacesnet.com/
All types of sales openings can be found here.

Medsearch America
www.medsearch.com/
Most of the job openings listed here are for practitioners, but they also occasionally list sales positions that are available.

VHA Sales Opportunities
www.vha.com/jobs/jobsales.htm
VHA is a group purchasing organization that also has sales positions that call on their members.

A noteworthy area of America Online features company profiles published by Plunkett Research, Ltd. These profiles provide overviews of each reviewed company as well as employee specifics such as salary and benefits. The Health Care Industry Almanac is especially appropriate since it highlights the top 500 companies in this business sector. This Plunkett publication is an outstanding reference work for job seekers in medical sales. Plunkett's works include:

Plunkett's Health Care Industry Almanac
Plunkett's Employer Almanacs
The Almanac of American Employers
Plunkett's InfoTech Industry Almanac

Gonyea and Associates
Attn: Worldwide Resume/Talent bank service
3543 Enterprise Road East
Safety Harbor, FL 34695

This company will assist you in getting your resume on the Internet and into several national recruiting databases.

PROFESSIONAL AND GOVERNMENT HEALTH CARE ORGANIZATIONS

The websites listed here will provide the job candidate with technical and statistical data relating to the health care field.

American Academy of Orthopedic Surgeons
www.aaos.org/

American Journal of Nursing
www.ajn.org/

American Medical Association
www.ama-assn.org/

American Nurses Association
www.nursingworld.org/

Association of Operating Room Nurses
www.aorn.org/

Centers for Disease Control
www.cdc.gov

Consumer Health Associations and Programs
www.hsc.missouri.edu/main_ndx/consumer.html

Consumer Health Information
www.nova.edu/Inter-Links/health/consumer.html

Health-Net
www.health.net

Health World Online
www.healthy.net

JCAHO
www.jcaho.org/

Medical Library Association
www.kumc.edu:80/MLA

Modern Healthcare
www.modernhealthcare.com/
Does list some sales openings

National Institute of Health
www.nih.gov

National Institute for Occupational Safety and Health
www.cdc.gov/niosh.htm

National Library of Medicine
www.nlm.nih.gov

NURSE
medsrv2.bham.ac.uk/nursing/

Nurse Week
www.nurseweek.com/

Occupational Safety and Health Administration
www.osha.gov

U.S. Department of Health and Human Services
www.os.dhhs.gov

U.S. Health Care Financing Adminstration
www.hcfa.gov/

World Health Organization
www.who.org/

SELECTED INTERESTING SITES

Sites that can provide market trends and health care education include:

Achoo—The Internet Health Care Directory
www.achoo.com/

Database of All U.S. Hospitals
www.medaccess.com/hospitals/s_hospt.htm

Database of U.S. Physicians
www.medaccess.com/physician/phys01.htm

The Digital Anatomist
www9.biostr.washington.edu/da.html

The Electric Apple Journal
www.lowellgeneral.org

This site is a "live" site, which features photos of surgery as it is being performed.

Indexes Thousands of Medical and Professional Journals
www.nlightn.com/

The Interactive Patient at Marshall University Medical School
medicus.marshall.edu/medicus.htm

Internet Resource Guide
www.aspenpub.com/internet/health.htm

A fantastic resource for all health-related sites.

Medical Matrix
www.slackinc.com/matrix/

A complete reference to clinical sites on the Internet.

Medscape
www.medscape.com/

MedWeb
www.emory.edu/WHSCL/medweb.html

Multimedia Medical Reference Library
www.med-library.com/

National Center for Health Statistics
www.cdc.gov/nchswww/nchshome.htm

Pharmaceutical Information Network
pharminfo.com/

Virtual Hospital
vh.radiology.uiowa.edu/

Voluntary Hospitals of America
www.vha.com/

ON-LINE SERVICES

America Online
8619 Westwood Center Drive
Vienna, VA 22182
800–827–6364

CompuServe
5000 Arlington Centre Boulevard
P.O. Box 20212
Columbus, OH 43220
800–848–8199

GEnie
c/o GE Information Services
P.O. Box 6403
Rockview, MD 20850
800–638–9636

Online Career Center
William Warren, Executive Director
3125 Dandy Trail
Indianapolis, IN 46214
317–293–6499
E-mail: Gopher.msen.com

Prodigy
445 Hamilton Avenue
White Plains, NY 10601
800–Prodigy

JOURNALS AND PERIODICALS

American Druggist
 1790 Broadway
 New York, NY 10019
 212–969–7500

American Journal of Infection Control
 11830 Westline Industrial Drive
 St. Louis, MO 63146-3318
 800–453–4351

American Journal of Nursing
 555 West Fifth-seventh Street
 New York, NY 10019
 212–582–8820

AORN Journal
 2170 South Parker Road
 Denver, CO 80231
 303–755–6300

Biomedical Products
 P.O. Box 650
 Morris Plains, NJ 07950

Contemporary Long-Term Care
 355 Park Avenue
 New York, NY 10010

Healthcare Executive
 840 North Lake Shore Drive
 Chicago, IL 60611

Healthcare Financial Management
Two Westbrook Corporate Center
Suite 700
Westchester, IL 60154
800–252–HFMA
708–531–9600

Healthcare Purchasing News
Two Northfield Plaza, Suite 300
Northfield, IL 60093-1217
847–441–3700

HIDA
1200 G Street, NW
Suite 400
Washington, DC 20005
202–783–8700

Home Healthcare Nurse
Lippincott-Raven Publishers
12107 Insurance Way
Hagerstown, MD 21740
800–638–3030

Hospitals and Health Networks
American Hospital Publishing, Inc.
737 North Michigan Avenue
Chicago, IL 60611
312–440–6800
800–621–6902
Hospitals@aol.com

Hospital Material Management Quarterly
Aspen Publishers, Inc.
7201 McKinney Circle
Frederick, MD 21701
800–638–8437
www.aspenpub.com

Infection Control & Sterilization Technology
Mayworm Associates, Inc.
507 North Milwaukee Avenue
Libertyville, IL 60048-2018

Journal of American Health Information Management Association
   919 North Michigan Boulevard, Suite 1400
   Chicago, IL 60611-1683
   312–787–2672
   www.ahima.org

Journal of the American Pharmaceutical Association
   2215 Constitution Avenue, NW
   Washington, DC 20037–2985
   202–628–4410

Medical Economics
   5 Paragon Drive
   Montvale, NJ 07645
   800–432–4570

Medical Industry Employment Opportunities
   Biomedical Market Newsletter Inc.
   3237 Idaho Place
   Costa Mesa, CA 92626-2207
   714–434–9500
   800–875–8181

Medical Product Sales
   Two Northfield Plaza, Suite 300
   Northfield, IL 60093-1217
   708–441–3700

Modern Healthcare
   740 Rush Street
   Chicago, IL 60606
   312–649–5341

Orthopedic Nursing
   National Association of Orthopedic Nurses
   East Holly Avenue, Box 56
   Pitman, NJ 08071-0056
   609–256–2310

Pharmaceutical Representative
   Two Northfield Plaza, Suite 300
   Northfield, IL 60093-1217
   847–441–3700
   800–451–7838

TRAINING COURSES FOR THE MEDICAL SALES REPRESENTATIVE

There are at least two independent sources that offer training for new medical sales representatives. These organizations are not affiliated with any company and can provide broad, general training for anyone wanting to become more knowledgeable in the field.

AORN Sales Professional Course
Rose Moss at Education Design
303–745–5996

This training program is designed to give representatives with no health care background an initial understanding of operating room techniques and an overview of selling to customers in the surgical environment.

The Certified Medical Representatives Institute
4950 Brambleton Avenue
Roanoke, VA 24018
800–274–2674

This training institute offers several continuing education programs for sales personnel in the pharmaceutical industry.

SELECTED MEDICAL FIELD COMPANIES

In order to provide the reader with a starting point, a few companies that specialize in the medical field are listed below. Additionally, three of the most thorough lists of health care related companies available are:

Health Industry Distributors Association Annual Directory
225 Reinekers Lane, Suite 350
Alexandria, VA 22314
703–549–4432

ORPD, 1996 OR Products Directory
AORN Customer Service
2170 S. Parker Road, Suite 300
Denver, CO 80231-5711
303–755–6300

Dun's Guide to Healthcare Companies
Dun's Marketing Service
3 Sylvan Way
Parsippany, NJ 07054
201–605–6000

The companies listed below were chosen because they are well recognized, national companies with sales forces made up of reps in nearly every state. This is not an exhaustive list but is intended to serve as a beginning point in your career search.

SELECTED PHARMACEUTICAL COMPANIES

Allergan, Inc.
P.O. Box 19534
Irvine, CA 92713
714–752–4500

Amgen
1840 DeHaviland Drive
Thousand Oaks, CA 91320
805–447–1000

Beecham, Inc.
1 Franklin Plaza
Philadelphia, PA 19102
215–751–4000

Boehringer Ingleheim Corp.
900 Ridgeway Road
Ridgefield, CT 06877
203–798–9988

Bristol Myers-Squibb
345 Park Avenue
New York, NY 10154-0037
212–546–4000

Burroughs Wellcome
3030 Cornwallis Road
Research Triangle Park, NC
27709
919–248–3000

Chiron
4560 Horton Street
Emeryville, CA 94608-2916
510–655–8730

Ciba-Geigy Corp.
444 Saw Mill River Road
Ardsley, NY 10502
914–479–5000

Eli Lilly & Company
Lilly Corporate Center
Indianapolis, IN 46285
317–276–2000

G.D. Searle & Co.
5200 Old Orchard Road
Skokie, IL 60077
708–982–7000

Glaxo, Inc.
5 Moore Drive
Research Triangle Park, NC
27709
919–248–2100

Hoechst Corp.
1041 U.S. Route
202-206 N.
Somerville, NJ 08807
908–231–2000

Hoffman-LaRoche, Inc.
340 Kingsland Street
Nutley, NJ 07110
201–235–5000

Marion Merrell Dow, Inc.
9300 Ward Parkway
Kansas City, MO 64114
816–966–4000

Merck & Co., Inc.
P.O. Box 100
Whitehouse Station, NJ
08889-0100
908–423–1000

Miles, Inc.
1127 Myrtle Street
Elkhart, IN 46515
219–264–8111

Ortho Pharmaceutical Corp.
Route 202, Box 300
Raritan, NJ 08869
201–218–6000

Pfizer, Inc.
235 East Forty-second Street
New York, NY 10017-5755
212–573–2323

Pharmacia & Upjohn Co.
7000 Portage Road
Kalamazoo, MI 49001
616–323–4000

Rhone-Poulene-Rorer
P.O. Box 1200
Collegeville, PA 19426
610–454–8000

Sandoz Pharmaceuticals Corp.
Route 10
East Hanover, NJ 07936
201–503–7500

Schering-Plough Corp.
1 Giralda Farms
Madison, NJ 07940-7000
201–822–7000

SmithKline Beecham Corp.
1 Franklin Plaza
Philadelphia, PA 19101
215–751–4000

Warner-Lambert Co.
201 Tabor Road
Morris Plains, NJ 07950
201–540–2000

Whitehall Laboratories
5 Giralda Farms
Madison, NJ 07940

Wyeth-Ayerst Laboratories
555 Lancaster Avenue
Radnor, PA 19087
215–688–4400

SELECTED MEDICAL COMPANIES

Abbott Laboratories
100 Abbott Park Road
Abbott Park, IL 60064
708–937–1511

Allergan, Inc.
2525 Dupont Drive
Irvine, CA 92715-1599
714–752–4500

Amsco International, Inc.
500 Grant Street
Pittsburgh, PA 15219
412–338–6500

Baxter Healthcare Corp.
1 Baxter Parkway
Deerfield, IL 60015
847–948–2000

Bausch & Lomb, Inc.
P.O. Box 54
Rochester, NY 14601-0054
716–338–6000

Becton Dickinson & Co.
1 Becton Drive
Franklin Lakes, NJ 07417-1880
201–847–6800

Bergen Brunswig
4000 Metropolitan Drive
Orange, CA 92668-3510
714–385–4000

Boston Scientific
1 Boston Scientific Place
Natick, MA 01760-1537
508–650–8000

C.R. Bard
730 Central Avenue
Murray Hill, NJ 07974
908–277–8000

General Medical Corporation
8741 Landmark Road
Richmond, VA 23228
804–264–7500

IVAX
8800 NW Thirty-sixth Street
Miami, FL 33178-2404
305–590–2200

Johnson & Johnson
1 Johnson & Johnson Plaza
New Brunswick, NJ 08933
908–524–0400

Kimberly-Clark Professional
Health Care
1400 Holcomb Bridge Road
Roswell, GA 30076
800–222–0126

Mallinckrodt Group
7733 Forsyth Boulevard
St. Louis, MO 63105
314–854–5200

Maxxim Medical
104 Industrial Boulevard
Sugar Land, TX 77478-3010
713–276–6107
800–462–9946

McKesson Corporation
One Post Street
San Francisco, CA 94104
415–983–9147
800–543–5857

Medtronic, Inc.
7000 Central Avenue, NE
Minneapolis, MN 55432-3576
612–574–4000

Owens & Minor
P.O. Box 27626
Richmond, VA 23261-7626
804–747–9794

Scimed Life Systems, Inc.
One Scimed Place
Maple Grove, MN 55311-1566
612–494–1700
800–832–7822

Spacelabs Medical Inc.
15220 Northeast Fortieth Street
Redmond, WA 98052-5305
206–885–4877
800–431–6967

St. Jude Medical, Inc.
1 Lillehi Plaza
St. Paul, MN 55117
612–483–2000

Sterile Concepts
5100 Commerce Road
Richmond, VA 23234-1091
804–275–0200
804–743–0535

Steris Corporation
9450 Pineneedle Drive
Mentor, OH 44060-1868
216–354–2600
800–628–3700

Stryker
P.O. Box 4085
Kalamazoo, MI 49003-4085
616–385–2600

U.S. Surgical Corp.
150 Glover Avenue
Norwalk, CT 06856
203–845–1000

RENNER LEARNING RESOURCE CENTER
ELGIN COMMUNITY COLLEGE
ELGIN, ILLINOIS 60123